MW01487501

Also by Mark C. Bodanza

A Game That Forged Rivals:
How Competition between Two New England High Schools
Created One of the Greatest Traditions in Football

1933

FOOTBALL AT THE DEPTH
OF THE GREAT DEPRESSION

MARK C. BODANZA

iUniverse, Inc.

New York   Bloomington

1933
Football at the Depth of the Great Depression

Copyright © 2010 Mark C. Bodanza

*All rights reserved. No part of this book may be used or reproduced by any means,
graphic, electronic, or mechanical, including photocopying, recording, taping or by any
information storage retrieval system without the written permission of the publisher
except in the case of brief quotations embodied in critical articles and reviews.*

iUniverse books may be ordered through booksellers or by contacting:

iUniverse
1663 Liberty Drive
Bloomington, IN 47403
www.iuniverse.com
1-800-Authors (1-800-288-4677)

*Because of the dynamic nature of the Internet, any Web addresses or links contained in this book
may have changed since publication and may no longer be valid. The views expressed in this work
are solely those of the author and do not necessarily reflect the views of the publisher, and the
publisher hereby disclaims any responsibility for them.*

ISBN: 978-1-4502-4523-4 (pbk)
ISBN: 978-1-4502-4524-1 (cloth)
ISBN: 978-1-4502-4525-8 (ebk)

Library of Congress Control Number: 2010932798

Printed in the United States of America

iUniverse rev. date: 9/8/10

For my dear, kind, and loving mother
Gloria Bodanza

Football is an emotional game. It must be played with enthusiasm and determination. To send a team on the field with this proper enthusiasm and determination is a coach's biggest problem. It is this task every week which causes him to walk the floor nights and talk to himself. He may have his team technically perfect in every detail but if he hasn't guessed right and developed the proper mental attitude his hours of effort on the field will be in vain.

—Lou Little, 1934

Contents

Preface

During the autumn of 2008, I began work on two projects. The first endeavor was coordinating an unscripted, competitive football game faithful to nineteenth-century style of play. This included sorting out the rules, locating equipment (barely more than a patchwork of period uniforms and a large watermelon-style football), and setting up the teams. No one, players, coaches, and myself included, knew what to expect.

The organizational details warranted the creation of a game program that very quickly became a book. Such abundant, complex planning could not be justly constrained to a limited treatment. *A Game That Forged Rivals* not only chronicles the 115-year history of the Massachusetts high school football rivalry of Leominster and Fitchburg, one of America's oldest, but also integrates that history with the story of our nation, the sport of football, and those who played the game. I didn't know what to expect from the book as I wrote it.

On a cold, rainy October day in 2009, the nineteenth-century football game was played before more than a thousand fans. One of those fans was Frank Novak, a local football legend recently retired after sixteen years of coaching experience in the National Football League. Frank's observations came in on the Monday following the game.

His comments were simple: "Of all the football games I've seen, I'll never forget that one."

The young men who played knew immediately afterward that they had been in, in every sense of the word, a battle. The ground shook, bodies collided, and yards were ground out with unrelenting battering, pushing, and pulling. True to the old style of play, and despite a requirement of only five yards for a first down instead of ten, the game ended in a 6–0 score, with Fitchburg the victor over Leominster.

Both winners and losers were satisfied. Their courage had been tested, and they all passed. They walked off the gridiron immediately understanding that they had just participated in something much bigger than themselves. An unbridled, collegial sharing of joy prevailed. It was as if combatants had emerged from the battlefield happy to have survived, immersed in immediate history, and with a newfound respect for their adversaries.

In anticipation of the pitched battle on the gridiron, *A Game That Forged Rivals* was published just a month before the game. The weeks following its release proved my editors correct: there was an interest in the Fitchburg-Leominster rivalry beyond the confines of central Massachusetts. The language of football is universal, as dozens of radio interviews revealed.

Everyone involved in both the game and the book had a story, a heartfelt memory, and a deep connection to the game. They shared their special recollection with sincere emotion, and I am greatly enriched by all the poignant and wonderful memories.

In the wake of those special days, this book was conceived. *1933: Football at the Depth of the Great Depression* recounts a remarkable year both on and off the football field. Over the past century of the American republic, 1933 rates as one of the most critical years, a time of historic crisis and change. The sport of football was impacted by the Great Depression in a variety of ways, some with lasting consequences.

Football creates some of the sporting world's most magical moments. From the very beginnings of the game, crowds have thrilled at the sight of outmatched, outsized teams wresting victory on the field. Sometimes the events of a dynamic world contribute to the drama. Participants can still tell the stories of 1933. Bill Mackie, a standout triple threat, is the sole surviving member of the 1933 Fitchburg High School team. Mackie's six foot three frame still displays marks of athleticism, nearly eight decades later. Others well into their nineties recollect the difficult year when America faced some of its biggest challenges. Joe Goodhue and Rick Cavaioli both played football on the 1932 Leominster High

School team and graduated in June 1933. They recall a year of worry, a time when work was a salve, not something to be avoided. It has been a true privilege to listen to these men, and my hope is to convey a sense of their times and the role football played in their lives.

When the notion of a nineteenth-century football game was introduced in 2009, many made mention of the era when football heroes donned leather helmets without facemasks, earning the players the nickname "leatherheads." In the 1890s, primitive leather helmets were a rare commodity. Many players relied on long hair alone for head protection. In 1933, leather helmets were standard. By the time this book is published in the fall of 2010, I hope that football fans in Fitchburg and Leominster will be able to witness a game played 1933 style. The '33 game will have a distinct advantage over the 1894 reenactment: This time, we will be honored by the presence of men who played the game nearly eight decades ago.

A Leominster player leaps to intercept a Fitchburg lateral in the 1894 reenactment game played October 24, 2009. Photograph by Vincent Apollonio, courtesy the *Leominster Champion*.

A Leominster player sweeps with Fitchburg players in close pursuit during the 1894 reenactment game in 2009. Photographed by Vincent Apollonio, courtesy the *Leominster Champion*.

Acknowledgments

The research and writing of history is often a solitary pursuit. But preparing the football history within these pages was anything but that. I have been truly blessed by a great deal of support as well as wonderful memories so generously shared by those with firsthand experiences. My first book, *A Game That Forged Rivals*, was released just before a historic football game, as this volume will precede the 1933 reenactment game in October 2010. In so many cases in the writing of this book, I learned that accomplishments on or off the gridiron were secondary to the human bonds, relationships, and amity created throughout the years. I am incredibly fortunate to have so many people share the depth of their connection to history and more importantly, the friends and teammates they shared it with.

I owe a primary debt of gratitude to Nancy Bell, a dear friend who provided great insight and critical analysis of the earliest drafts of the manuscript. Thank you to my editorial consultant, Kathi Wittkamper, for her expertise and genuine support. Linda Pinder of the Leominster Historical Society helped in numerous ways, including lending her incredible talents toward the creation and restoration of images. Thank you to Adrian Nicole LeBlanc, an author herself, for being a great mentor and friend.

I am deeply grateful to Bill Mackie, Joe Goodhue, and Rick Cavaioli, three great men who played the game in the early 1930s and contributed a wonderful collection of memories about an era when difficulty brought out the best in people. Sandra and Jerry Belliveau contributed memories and photos of Ronnie Cahill, Sandra's father. I am also grateful to Father James Callahan of St. Anna Church, with whom I happily shared the joys of the game, and who has inspired me in the most important of ways. A number of friends not only encouraged this book, but wholeheartedly supported the effort to recreate some amazing historic football. I thank Brian Montaquila, Peter Angelini, Tom McNamara, Andy Rome, and Dick O'Brien. Frank Novak, a Leominster native with sixteen years of NFL coaching under his belt, was and is a great source of inspiration who generously contributed his wealth of experience.

A number of men, with combined coaching experience that would eclipse the entire 116-year history of the Leominster-Fitchburg rivalry, helped bring nineteenth-century football to life in 2009. Marcos Meza, Michael Austin, Ronald "Togo" Palazzi, Richard Mazzaferro, and Ralph Jacques deserve gratitude for ably executing the not-so-simple task of fielding an 1894 football team. Larry Bizzotto not only coached but played in the game. He and Peter Angelini, each of whom are over age fifty, were courageous to enter a fray dominated by younger and, in many cases, larger men. Gil Donatelli, the head coach of the Leominster team, was and continues to be one of the greatest supporters of this entire endeavor. I owe him a special thank-you for a multitude of contributions that have made the playing of historic football possible and these books better.

My research was facilitated by many kind people who cooperated with the greatest interest and encouragement. Thank you to Susan Shelton of the Leominster Library, Jane Fischer, Sandy Balboni, the Leominster Historical Society, Susan Roetzer, and the Fitchburg Historical Society. The gentlemen at the Leominster Historical Commission, including Dave Chester, Don Piermarini, Robert Saudelli, Rocco Palmeri, Chet Carter, and Leon Christoforo, were happy to assist in my review of their football history collection.

Many others helped in important ways: from Leominster Access Television, Jack Celli and Carl Piermarini; the mayors, Lisa Wong of Fitchburg and Leominster's Dean Mazzarella; from the Leominster Department of Public Works, Director, Patrick LaPointe; from Leominster Emergency Management, Charles Coggins, Debbie Consalvo, and their dedicated volunteers.

From the football programs, there are others to thank: Leominster head coach John Dubzinski and athletic director Christopher Young. Fitchburg's two-way head coach and athletic director, Ray Cosenza, honored me with the privilege of addressing his team just before its last practice in preparation for the all important Thanksgiving contest, something I never imagined as an LHS alumnus.

A tireless supporter of Leominster's football youth, Joe DeCarolis was a significant and unheralded supporter. Joe, who like his father was a center for Leominster, was also the team's long snapper. He may be responsible for the team's most important long snap. He initiated a field goal try that Frank Novak, Jr. converted to defeat Fitchburg by a score of 3–0 in overtime, a win that preserved an undefeated season in 1978. No one ever notices the long snapper until he makes a mistake.

My law office staff, Kathleen Welch and Gabriella Goodale, were of great assistance. My brother and law partner David Bodanza was patient and helpful. I am blessed to have him as a brother.

To my wife Adele and children, Melissa, Kathryn, and Nicholas, I give my love and appreciation for their patience, understanding, and support. Last but not least, to the newest member of the family, grandson Brody: you have already inspired me in more ways than you will ever know.

Introduction

The low point of the Great Depression came in 1933, an extraordinary year for that reason and others. The impact of the financial crisis was most sorely felt by the nation that year. Americans' faith in their government and financial institutions was shaken like never before. Political leaders attempted to persuade the nation that confidence in America and its economy was not only necessary but patriotic. The country's highest law enforcement figures tried to convince their fellow citizens that murdering, bank-robbing gangsters were not folk heroes but dangerous felons. Deprivation and scarcity frightened Americans, all of whom wanted the opportunity promised by the American dream, or at least a place at the table.

In the midst of the chaos, the nation needed diversions and entertainment more than ever. One peculiarly American game, football, provided at least a momentary escape from daily cares and worries. Football was played with vigor in 1933. The sport had grown in popularity since the 1880s, when Walter Camp introduced sufficient modifications to England's Rugby Union rules to create a new American sport.

In 1933, the gridiron itself was a theatre of change that in some ways mirrored the pace of transformations in American society. The sport weathered the Depression at every level, from the sandlot and high schools to the professional game. In the latter case, the alterations were a mixed bag. Both positive and negative developments spawned by the Depression impacted the sport for decades to come.

The Depression slowed a growing movement to reform the financial structure of big-time college football. Dwindling gate receipts and cash-strapped alumni could no longer afford to fund a sport that increasingly relied on the recruitment of talented players with financial inducements. The practical effect of the Depression on football made institutional changes seem, at least for a time, unnecessary. Despite the dearth of cash, enthusiasm for the game did not abate. The culmination of the 1933 college football season was one of the most exciting Rose Bowls ever played. 1933 was the last year that the "granddaddy of them all" was the only postseason college football bowl game.

The high school game was an important part of life in communities across America. The observance of established traditions helped prevent the thread of the American fabric from fraying during the days of economic and social tumult. A robust, well-established high school football rivalry was, as it is today, one of the strongest traditions in towns across the country.

Two cities located in north-central Massachusetts, Fitchburg and Leominster, started their 1933 football seasons with great hope. The two teams played tough schedules, featuring games against some of the most powerful high school teams in eastern Massachusetts, New Hampshire, and Rhode Island.

The Fitchburg and Leominster football Warriors entered each of their 1933 games encouraged by the unbridled optimism of their steadfast fans. Their supporters hoped for victory in each of the many significant challenges. One game more than all the rest provided the ultimate measure of success for each squad. No team can be truly satisfied with its performance unless they beat their archrival. Never was this more true than when Leominster and Fitchburg played on Thanksgiving Day 1933.

The two Massachusetts teams traced their rivalry back to 1894. In the prior thirty-nine seasons the teams had played each other forty-nine times, each of the games an autumn highlight in the area. But 1933 was different. The game never had such significance. Recounting a football season faded by the passage of nearly eight decades may be more important than recounting last year's season. The time approaches when any memory of that fabled year will not be a firsthand account; there are few participants still living. Those still surviving deserve our ear just as much as the compelling history of their time merits telling.

When a century sets on 1933, future Americans will attempt to understand a time when America survived. In the struggle of those days we can find hope that each new challenge faced by the nation might prompt the same resolve that Americans showed in the darkest days of the Great Depression.

—— *Chapter 1:* ——

A Nation's Hope

Morning sun and mild temperatures bathed Doyle Field as the Leominster and Fitchburg football squads prepared for their traditional holiday game. In 1933, Thanksgiving came as late in November as possible. November 30 was the last Thursday of the month.[1] Each team wore silk football pants; Fitchburg donned red, and Leominster blue. The fabric shimmered. Ten thousand fans waited in anticipation; partisans crowding the grandstands. Leominster's blue and white dominated the north side, and a throng of red-and-gray-cloaked Fitchburg fans occupied the opposite seats. Earthen embankments that sloped toward

---

1   Most states, including Massachusetts, observed the holiday as proclaimed by Abraham Lincoln in 1863, on November's last Thursday. 1933 was the last year the nation officially celebrated Thanksgiving on the last Thursday of November. It was the next to the last time Massachusetts would. President Franklin Roosevelt sought to regularize the holiday observance on the fourth Thursday of the month, when the calendar yielded a fifth November Thursday in 1939. Depression-battered merchants could not afford a shorter holiday shopping season resulting from a late Thanksgiving. Massachusetts was one of a number of states which failed to follow the President's proclamation. The anomaly of states celebrating the holiday on different dates was eliminated when Congress legislated Thanksgiving as the fourth Thursday of November in December 1941.

each end zone accommodated another three thousand fans for whom there were no seats.

It was the fortieth year of the rivalry between the two central Massachusetts schools. No one could remember a more important game. The match was billed as a pinnacle of the rivalry, a game of games. 1933 was proving a momentous year both on and off the football field.

The nation was in the midst of an economic collapse, ultimately called the Great Depression. The depth of despair felt earned the panic a singular place in the history of American financial turmoil. The Great Depression was preceded by an age of contradictions. The twenties were years of innocence, unbridled optimism, and technological advance. That decade saw the mass production of the automobile, transatlantic telephone service, and a rapid electrification of the country's landscape. It was also a time of excess and wild speculation, filled with bootleggers intent on quenching the thirst of a nation bristling against Prohibition.

When the stock markets crashed on October 29, 1929—"Black Tuesday"—Americans were caught off-guard. The decline was rapid and precipitous. Bank failures rose from 659 in 1929 to 2,294 in 1931. Nearly one-third of American workers were without a job by the winter of 1933.[2] Bank holidays were declared to stem the streams of frightened depositors seeking to withdraw their savings. Hunger haunted every corner of the nation.

The crisis required leadership to protect the American psyche. Ironically, the impoverished looked to a man of privilege in the presidential elections of November 1932. The president-elect, Franklin Delano Roosevelt, faced a huge challenge. Despite the advantages of an education at Groton, Harvard, and Columbia Law School, FDR knew adversity. Stricken by polio in 1921, he required the aid of crutches or a wheelchair for the rest of his life. The press shielded his physical disability from public view.

Even before his illness, Roosevelt demonstrated determination in the face of inauspicious circumstances. His years at Groton were marked by a lack of athletic prowess, an ingredient necessary for real distinction at the school. The headmaster, Endicott Peabody, believed sport integral to maturation and football was at the top of his list. To Walter Camp,

---

2   Brinkley, *History of the United States*, 402.

"father of American Football," Peabody wrote, "I am convinced that football is of profound importance for the moral even more than the physical development of the boys." The smallish Roosevelt, who lacked any experience in team sports, found a place on the second worst of eight football teams at the school.[3] Perhaps Peabody was correct. FDR never forgot his boyhood days at Groton, the lessons learned both in and out of the classroom. He drew on those experiences early in his presidency.

The first one hundred days of Roosevelt's administration produced a dizzying array of legislative initiatives aimed to right the American economy and establish an equitable distribution of wealth. Government grew quickly, and new agencies emerged, known by acronyms still familiar today. Virtually lost to history is the fact that the whole program almost ended before it ever got off the ground.

On February 15, 1933, the president-elect visited Miami to address a convention of Legionnaires. Roosevelt delivered his speech seated on the top of the back seat of an open car. Roosevelt conversed with Chicago mayor Anton Cermak after the public talk concluded. Cermak, who had supported FDR's primary Democratic Party rival, Al Smith, was in Miami to court the president-elect's assistance for Chicago's ailing school district, which could not afford to pay its teachers. Just forty feet away stood Giuseppe Zangara, a thirty-two-year-old Italian bricklayer. The despondent Zangara had a disdain for the elite. Suddenly, he raised a revolver purchased in a North Miami pawnshop for eight dollars. Five shots were quickly discharged. The assassin's aim was disrupted when Mrs. Lillian Cross instinctively hit his arm with her handbag. Roosevelt was spared by a matter of inches. Cermak was not. The Chicago mayor was critically wounded and died on March 6, just two days after FDR was inaugurated as America's thirty-second president.[4]

Zangara was unrepentant. At his trial he testified, "The capitalists killed my life. I suffer, always suffer. I make it fifty-fifty—someone else must suffer." When asked if he wanted to live, the assassin replied, "No. Put me in the electric chair." He had no remorse. His only sorrow was

---

3   Smith, *FDR*, 28.
4   Smith, *FDR*, 297.

in failing to kill Roosevelt. One of Zangara's wishes was indulged when he was executed on March 20, 1933.[5]

By all accounts, Roosevelt was fearless throughout the whole ordeal. Those who were with him in the hours just after the assassination attempt found him unfazed. Raymond Moley, a Columbia University political science professor who was assisting with policymaking and speechwriting, was impressed. "I have never in my life seen anything more magnificent than Roosevelt's calm that night ..."[6] This courage would prove essential to the first few weeks of Roosevelt's administration. Circumstances were dire in the spring of 1933.

During his relatively brief inauguration speech, Roosevelt called for God's guidance on a number of occasions. Earlier that morning he established a precedent by attending a prayer service. Roosevelt told his soon-to-be Postmaster General James Farley that "I think a thought to God is the right way to start off my administration."[7] Reverend Endicott Peabody of the Groton School presided over the service, which included readings from the Book of Common Prayer. Roosevelt selected the hymns "Faith of Our Fathers" and "O God, Our Help in Ages Past." During the speech itself, the new president famously declared to the millions listening by radio around the nation:

> This great nation will endure as it has endured, and will revive and will prosper. So, first of all, let me assert my firm belief that the only thing we have to fear is fear itself—nameless, unreasoning, unjustified terror which paralyzes needed efforts to convert retreat into advance.[8]

The inaugural address resonated with a public seeking confidence in government, and perhaps more importantly, hope.

FDR acted quickly. On his first full day as president, he proclaimed a national bank holiday to stem disarray in the financial sector of the economy. His second proclamation on March 5 called Congress back into session. More action followed just as decisively though not without

---

5   *New York Times*. March 21, 1933.
6   Smith, *FDR*, 298.
7   Farley, *Behind The Ballots*, 208.
8   Roosevelt, *2 Public Papers and Addresses*, 11-16.

considerable deliberation. FDR saw himself as a quarterback. During a press conference on April 13, 1933, he said:

> It is a little bit like a football team that has a general game plan against the other side. Now the captain and the quarterback of that team know pretty well what the next play is going to be and they know the general strategy for the team; but they can not tell you what the play after the next is going to be until the next play is run off. If the play makes few yards, the succeeding play will be different from what it would have been if they had been thrown for a loss. I think that is the easiest way to explain it.[9]

FDR's use of a football metaphor to describe his new administration's approach to the Depression was ironic, as the sport itself was on the threshold of change. 1933 was a year of great uncertainty. Not all of the decisions made during these uncertain days would be wise ones.

---

9   Smith, *FDR*, 308.

— Chapter 2: —

Barrier of Shame

Leominster had welcomed black athletes to the gridiron for as long as anyone can remember. The handful of African-American families living in Leominster during the first half of the twentieth century contributed mightily to the fortunes of Leominster High School football. The Hazards, Chesters, Munroes, and Dupees sent a number of talented young men to the field. As early as 1928, Charlie Hazard not only played for Leominster but served as his team's captain.[10]

When the Leominster and Fitchburg football players began their campaigns in 1933, race relations in America were not on their young minds. The same could not be said of their forebears. Both communities had hosted abolitionist activity as early as the 1840s. Each town maintained stops on the Underground Railroad, and both drew the rebuke of President Millard Fillmore after residents helped rescue the fugitive slave Shadrach Minkins in February 1851.

The Minkins case was the first to arise in New England after the passage of a new fugitive slave law, one feature of a legislative package

---

10 The Chesters alone fielded five brothers (Dick, George, Dave, Bob, and Peter), all of whom played for Leominster High School between 1943 and 1960. A sixth brother, Gerry, played at a parochial high school in Fitchburg. Interview with David Chester, March 15, 2010.

championed by Senators Daniel Webster of Massachusetts and Henry Clay of Kentucky. The Compromise of 1850 was predicated more on the notion of saving the union than principle. Fugitive slave cases were removed from state jurisdiction and the sympathy of Northern juries. New cases were brought before federal commissioners who were paid five dollars if a fugitive slave was freed and ten if the runaway was sent back to slavery. Minkins's hearing before a commissioner was averted when a group of free blacks in Boston stormed the courthouse and spirited the prisoner away.[11] After Underground Railroad stops in Dorchester and Concord, Minkins arrived in Leominster at the home of Jonathan and Frances Drake. After spending an evening with the Drakes, he was transported to the West Fitchburg home of Benjamin Snow before booking passage on a train through Vermont and into Canada and freedom.

On February 19, 1851, President Fillmore, at the urging of Webster, issued a proclamation in response to the Minkins case, calling for Massachusetts citizens to obey the law and respect all military and civil authority. Furthermore, Fillmore called for the prosecution of those persons who aided or abetted the "flagitious offense."[12] Of all the conspirators, Frances Drake of Leominster was the boldest and least deterred. A committed abolitionist, she had hosted some of the greatest anti-slavery notables in her Franklin Street home during the two decades before the Civil War. Her callers included William Lloyd Garrison, Wendell Phillips, and Frederick Douglass. Notably Mrs. Drake supported women's rights, a notion that placed her in the minority even among fellow reformers.[13] Even more pointedly, Mrs. Drake fervently believed in racial integration, an idea not supported by the vast majority of abolitionists. In an 1843 letter to Maria Chapman Weston of Boston, Drake expressed the following:

> One lady to test my principles ask(ed) me if I would marry a coloured man: I answered very frankly (as my mother ever prompted) yes—if he was as worthy in

---

11 Collison, *Shadrach Minkins*, 127.
12 Collison, *Shadrach Minkins*, 140.
13 Bodanza, *The Coming Crucible*, 16.

every respect as a white man ought to be. You have no
idea what a talk it has made all over town.[14]

Ninety years later in 1933, the owners of the fledgling National
Football League were not interested in racial integration. In fact a
movement was afoot to segregate the thirteen-year-old league. The
reasons for segregation were transparent. Some owners feared that their
fans might share their bigotry and reject the idea of black players taking
positions away from whites. Why this regrettable course of prejudice
was followed by all the team owners is not entirely clear.

Black players were not numerous in the NFL before 1933.
Nonetheless, their contributions were significant. Fritz Pollard of
the Akron Professionals played and served as his team's head coach
between 1920 and 1926. In the first year of the league, Pollard, a star
running back, led Akron to an undefeated season and the first NFL
championship. In the years between 1920 and 1933, a dozen other black
players accomplished much in the face of adversity and prejudice.[15] In
1933, all that changed.

In that pivotal year, George Preston Marshall, a native of Washington
DC, became the majority owner of the NFL's Boston Redskins. Marshall
was a segregationist. Unfortunately, he was persuasive as well. Marshall
brought improvements to the game, among them the formation of two
divisions and a championship game featuring the top team from each
division. The Redskins owner worked closely on league improvements
with the owner of the Chicago Bears, George Halas. In February 1933,
the pair implemented rule changes that promoted more scoring and
excitement, changes that would boost the NFL's fortunes in the future.
Sadly, they also established a color barrier in professional football.

One explanation for the actions of Marshall, Halas, and the other
owners, beyond base bigotry, involved jobs and the Depression. Some
theorized that owners believed that white fans would disapprove of blacks
competing for jobs with white players. Whatever their motivations,

---

14 Drake, *Letter to Maria Chapman Weston*, 4.
15 Recognition of Pollard's achievements in the early years of the NFL came
with his posthumous election to the Hall of Fame in 2005. Sabol, *The
Leaders: Breaking Racial Barriers in the NFL*, DVD.

there is no satisfactory explanation for the unfortunate stain on NFL history.[16]

The NFL passed its first thirteen years, if not fully integrated, then at least not prohibiting black players. Its second thirteen years featured no black players. In 1946, the curtain of shame began to lift. Two professional teams led the way. One belonged to the NFL and the other to the new All-America Football Conference (AAFC). One team adopted change willingly and the other transfigured itself of necessity.

One year before Branch Rickey famously signed Jackie Robinson to a Brooklyn Dodgers' contract, beginning the integration of baseball, the Cleveland Rams were on the move. The Rams' owner had received permission from the league to leave Cleveland for Los Angeles. The move was motivated in part by competition with the AAFC which planned to establish a franchise in Los Angeles owned by actor Don Ameche. The new team was to bear the name "Dons." Both the Rams and the Dons were competing for a lease to play at the same venue, the Los Angeles Coliseum.

The Los Angeles Coliseum Commission, a public agency, operated the Coliseum. The commission held a hearing on January 15, 1946 to evaluate the two proposals. In attendance was William "Hally" Harding, a prominent member of the local black community. Over nearly two decades, Harding compiled a résumé of sporting accomplishments that included participation in college football as well as black-only baseball and football leagues. Harding went before the commission at the request of thirty colored newspapers. The official record does not include Harding's remarks. Witnesses suggested that he was persuasive. Commissioner Roger Jessue rose to speak. His mind turned to UCLA football star Kenny Washington, whose race precluded him from a place in the NFL. Washington was twenty-eight by 1946, a member of the LAPD. He also starred on the gridiron as a member of the Hollywood Bears of the Pacific Coast Football League. Jessue made it plain: "If our Kenny Washington can't play, there will be no pro football in the L.A. Coliseum."[17]

The Rams' management was cornered. The team was forced to concede that Washington and a number of black athletes would not be

---

16 Piascik, *The Best Show in Football*, 35.
17 Wolff, *Sports Illustrated*, Volume III, No. 14, October 12, 2009.

ineligible to play for the Rams. In the spring of 1946, the Rams signed the NFL's first two black players in thirteen years. Kenny Washington signed first, followed by Woody Strode, a teammate of Washington's at UCLA. The road ahead was not easy for the two. These football pioneers encountered widespread prejudice and resistance from other players, owners, and the public. Taunts, segregated facilities, and threats met black professionals wherever they traveled. Strode summed it up when he said, "If I have to integrate heaven, I don't want to go."[18] While the Rams of the NFL were essentially coerced to integrate, the circumstances with the AAFC franchise in Cleveland were different.

Cleveland's AAFC franchise, the Browns, bore the name of its coach and general manager Paul Brown. Brown was singular in purpose: He intended to field the very best football team possible and little would get in his way. Race was not a roadblock to his objective. Legendary running back Jim Brown said Paul Brown "integrated football the right way …" According to the star,

> Paul Brown integrated pro football without uttering a single word about integration. He just went out, signed a bunch of great black athletes, and started kicking butt. That's how you do it. You don't talk about it. Paul never said a word about race.[19]

If Paul Brown was color-blind, Branch Rickey of the Brooklyn Dodgers was not. It is no accident that the story of Jackie Robinson is so well-known and the account of the great black athletes who integrated football is not. Rickey was making a statement. His motivations are the subject of speculation. Paul Brown's goal was simply to win.

In 1943, Bill Willis was the first African-American at Ohio State to earn All-American honors. Willis, a tackle, was coached by the future Cleveland Browns coach Paul Brown during Ohio State's 1942 championship season.[20] Willis knew that playing in the NFL was not in his future. He didn't resent the lack of opportunity. It just wasn't part of Bill Willis's makeup to resent anything. After college, Willis served as the head football coach of Kentucky State for a year. When

---

18 Wolff, *Sports Illustrated*, Volume III, No. 14, October 12, 2009.
19 Piascik, *The Best Show in Football*, 32.
20 *New York Times*, November 29, 2007.

his former coach founded the Browns, Willis drove to Cleveland to investigate the possibility of playing professional football in the AAFC. Brown informed his former player that nothing precluded his playing in the league and that he would get back to him. According to Willis, "he never did."

Willis persisted. He showed up at the Browns' training camp in August 1946 on his own dime. The next day he was on the training field displaying amazing strength and quickness from the defensive middle guard position. The established centers, including starter Mo Scarry, simply could not stop Willis. The matchups attracted the attention of the Browns' coaches and players, especially Paul Brown.[21] On August 7, 1946 Bill Willis signed a professional football contract with a starting salary of $4,000.[22] Thirty-one years later he would be inducted into the NFL's Hall of Fame. Just three days after the Willis contract, the Browns signed Marion Motley, a bruising, six-foot-two fullback who weighed 235 pounds.[23] Together, the Rams' Washington and Strode and the Browns' Willis and Motley were the first African-Americans to integrate a major professional sport, a year before Jackie Robinson made his famous entry into major league baseball.

---

21 Piascik, *The Best Show in Football*, 36-37.

22 *USA Today*, November 21, 2006.

23 Piascik, *The Best Show in Football*, 40-43.

— *Chapter 3:* —

The Game Reshaped

On May 27, 1933, the Century of Progress opened in Chicago. It was the second world's fair hosted by the Windy City. In 1893, the Columbian Exposition celebrated the four-hundredth anniversary of Columbus's exploration of the Americas, albeit a year behind schedule.[24] The city's second exposition was originally intended to celebrate Chicago's past. The theme changed in the wake of the Great Depression, an era of gangster violence and threats to social order.

The Century of Progress came to symbolize the cooperation between science, industry, and government. Before the fair closed on October 31, 1934, more than forty million Americans were treated to its vision of the country's future. Streamlined surfaces and bright colors set the tone for change. President Roosevelt and industrial leaders saw the fair as an opportunity to strengthen confidence in the nation's economic future. Spending and modernizing were recurrent themes. A model home conceived by George Keck was billed as "the House of Tomorrow." The futuristic abode was constructed with a number of synthetic building

---

24 The 1893 fair featured nine pavilions constructed by various American corporations. Fitchburg's Simond Saw & Steel Company maintained the largest exhibit at the fair. Kirkpatrick, *The City and the River*, 390.

products. Its designers predicted that some day automatic dishwashers and air conditioning would become widely available.[25]

The fair quickly rose to national prominence. Its messages were vital and timely. President Roosevelt was thoroughly convinced that the Century of Progress was a valuable complement to the many programs of the New Deal, a comprehensive package of government reforms including public investment in the private sector, all of which sought to restore America's confidence. The president convinced the fair's organizers to extend it through 1934. Faith in the American economy was invaluable. Faith and belief in the future went hand in hand during 1933. More than ever, the future meant change.

America's institutions were reconsidered during the Great Depression. Sports were not immune to refinement. Football adopted a number of changes in 1933. As seen in the previous chapter, not all were positive. Nevertheless, some changes were for the betterment of the game. Football, specifically the NCAA, which was the rules authority for the college and high school game, was in an introspective mood.

Members of the official football rules committee were ever mindful of the game's prospects. William R. Okeson, who edited *Spalding's Official Football Rules of the National Collegiate Athletic Association*, wondered about the direction of the sport.

> We are all wondering what that future will be, and most of us become slightly bemused when we try to visualize it. Be sure of one thing: that foot ball will follow, in the future as it has in the past, that national trend. If that trend is materialistic, foot ball will be so also; but if the nation manifests a broader sportsmanship in its ideas and actions; that same sportsmanship will be apparent in foot ball. We congratulate ourselves on the advance college foot ball has made in recent years. Certainly it is better conducted, with little trace of rowdyism. Its strategy and technique are far superior to that of the old game. Intersectional games have allayed much of the jealousy that once existed as between different sections of the country. Coaching and officiating have become

---

25 *Official Guide Book of the World's Far 1934*, 170.

better and more uniform. The game in every way is more colorful and enjoyable. Yet we should not shut our eyes to certain tendencies, which are not as helpful or hopeful as they might be. Too much emphasis is placed on the actions and personalities of rules makers, coaches and athletic directors. Too little attention is given to the enjoyment the players get out of the game. There is a lot of folderol about the educational value of foot ball, when its real value is the sheer joy the player who loves it gets from skillfully playing it. The truth is that the game has become too artificial and complex to be played without the aid of meticulous rules making, clever coaching and efficient officiating. There is a lot of machinery required to produce a foot ball team, and unless that machinery produces a flawless product there is weeping, wailing and gnashing of teeth.[26]

Okeson's role in the NCAA expanded in 1933. The chairman of the football rules committee, Edward Kimball Hall, died at Hanover, New Hampshire on November 10, 1932. The committee's secretary, William S. Langford, delivered the annual report in Hall's stead at the Hotel Astor in New York on December 30. Okeson succeeded Hall as chairman of the important rules committee.[27] The man from whom Okeson took the reins was a thoughtful guardian of the game. Hall, years before his death, compiled a list of evils he believed football should avoid. These included:

1. Overemphasis of the individual player, as seen in pre-season press notices, glorification and the like.
2. The danger of not keeping professional foot ball and college foot ball distinctly and definitely separated.
3. Overemphasis of the necessity of having a winning season.

---

26 Okeson, *Spalding's Official Football Rules of the National Collegiate Athletic Association 1933*, 8. (Note: the spelling of "foot ball" is consistent with the convention of the time and is preserved as in the original.)
27 Okeson, *Spalding's Official Football Rules of the National Collegiate Athletic Association 1933*, 17.

4. The tendency to treat the winning of games as a business rather than a sport.[28]

Clean and safe competition devoid of the corrupting forces of big business had been a primary objective for many years prior to 1933. The pivotal 1905 college football season, which was marked by nineteen player deaths, was a year of crisis that led to major changes in 1906, not the least of which was the forward pass. The pass and sixteen other changes saved the game from near abolishment. The new rules were intended to open the game up and avoid a tighter, massed, battering style of play.[29]

The annual report delivered by Langford in December 1932 and published in *Spalding's 1933 Guide* listed twenty-one deaths in all of football from the professional game to the sandlot during 1931. The committee estimated a mortality rate of less than three one-hundredths of 1 percent, when taking into consideration the participation of 750,000 estimated players.[30] Neither the 1933 guide, which claimed the injury reports for 1932 were still being tabulated nor the 1934 guide, reported the 1932 injuries and deaths. Langford concluded his report regarding 1932, as follows:

> The number of serious and fatal injuries which have been reported by the press as occurring during the season of 1932 is disconcerting at the moment, as it was confidently expected that the changes in rules which were effected last February would bring about a much lower average, and, although there has been

---

28 Okeson, *Spalding's Official Football Rules of the National Collegiate Athletic Association 1933*, 17.

29 Bodanza, *A Game That Forged Rivals*, 91-96.

30 In 1905, a staggering number of football players died from injuries suffered on the gridiron. Some estimates of player deaths, which included collegiate, interscholastic, and club football players across the country, ranged as high as one hundred. Whatever the debate there might be over the statistics, it is clear that at least nineteen of America's young men died playing intercollegiate football in 1905. The grim statistics were made worse when journalists brought to light the intentional nature of some on-field violence. Bodanza, *A Game That Forged Rivals*, 91.

a material decrease from last season, the casualty list as reported must be regarded as a problem of serious import. From the preliminary information at hand, it appears that by far the larger percentage of these accidents occurred in high school and sandlot games— in direct ratio to the lack of supervision exercised— and that but three cases resulting fatally occurred in colleges holding membership in this Association. The inquiry into the causes of accidents and the details, not only of each occurrence itself but of the antecedent circumstances and the subsequent medical or surgical treatment, is being carried on with utmost efficiency by a Committee for the Study of Safety in College Physical Education under the auspices of the School of Education of New York University. Separate reports are being prepared by the Rules Committee itself, by the American Foot Ball Coaches Association under the able direction of Dr. Stevens, and by Mr. Fielding H. Yost, Physical Director of the University of Michigan. As soon as the data has been collected and tabulated, these reports will be made available to the members of next year's Rules Committee, which will not hesitate to apply such remedies as in its judgment seem warranted by the conclusions arrived at. In the meantime it is only fair that judgment should be withheld until, after mature and deliberate consideration of the facts, proper solutions may be reached.[31]

The 1933 rules committee made only minor changes for the 1934 season. That was not the case the year before. The preceding committee made a number of significant rule changes that impacted the 1933 season favorably. Unlike 1931 and 1932, there were no deaths reported in 1933 for any of the nation's varsity college football teams.[32] The 1933

---

31 Okeson, *Spalding's Official Football Rules of the National Collegiate Athletic Association 1933*, 19.

32 Okeson, *Spalding's Official Football Rules of the National Collegiate Athletic Association 1934*, 9.

rule amendments considered the most significant by contemporaries included:

1. The prohibition of the use of certain equipment deemed dangerous, and the requirement that legal equipment must be padded to avoid injury to opponents.
2. Banning the massing of the team receiving the kick-off by requiring at least five players to remain near the center of the field until the ball was kicked.
3. The prohibition of the flying block and the flying tackle.
4. The liberalization of the substitution rule so as to permit an injured or tired player to be withdrawn once each quarter and returned to the game in any subsequent period.
5. The amendment of the dead-ball rule so as to provide that when any portion, except hands or feet, of the player in possession of the ball touches the ground, the ball was to be ruled dead automatically.
6. The further restriction of the use of hands and arms by players on defense in contact with the heads, necks, or faces of opponents.[33]

Worthy of note is the concept that certain equipment might be dangerous. Interestingly, some commentators make that same claim in the context of modern professional football. In 1933, concerns regarding dangerous protective equipment were governed by Rule 5, Section 3 of the NCAA rules. Today players routinely wear yards of tape to support ankles, wrists, and hands. Taping of hands, except to protect an injury, was prohibited in 1933. Any player who had his hands taped was required to report to the umpire prior to the game for special permission to play. Taping of the wrists, devoid of any offensive purpose, was legal and did not require advance screening. All players were required to wear soft knee guards. Thigh and shin guards made of a "hard or unyielding substance" were required to be "padded on the whole outside surface

---

33 Okeson, *Spalding's Official Football Rules of the National Collegiate Athletic Association 1933*, 18.

and overlapping on edges with felt, foam rubber or other soft padding, at least 3/8 of an inch in thickness."[34]

Even the use of cleats was highly regulated. Leather, rubber, or other non-metallic cleats were allowed providing that the tips of conical projections were not less than 3/8" in diameter. Oblong cleats were to be no less than 1/4" by 3/4". Any player found with objectionable equipment was subject to suspension unless the offending item or items was corrected within two minutes.[35]

The rule also made a plea regarding the leather helmet in 1933. Section 2 concluded as follows:

Special Note

The Committee recommends that head protections or helmets be worn by all players and urgently requests that coaches assume primary responsibility for the use of equipment, which may be dangerous.

In addition to voicing concerns regarding the potential dangers of equipment, the NCAA also took pains to insure that equipment did not provide any team or player an unfair competitive advantage. Deception was a big part of the game during the 1930s. Some legendary trick plays involving hidden ball gimmicks and players hiding out of bounds while awaiting a pass were still fresh on the minds of rule makers.[36]

---

34 Okeson, *Spalding's Official Football Rules of the National Collegiate Athletic Association 1933*, 19.

35 Okeson, *Spalding's Official Football Rules of the National Collegiate Athletic Association 1933*, 19.

36 One of the most dramatic of trick plays was employed by the Carlisle School's legendary coach Pop Warner in 1907 during the early days of the forward pass. In a game against Chicago, Carlisle's end sprinted for the sideline and out of bounds. Albert Exendine ran behind his school's band and twenty-five yards down the field still out of bounds and undetected. When he finally reentered the field of play, the Carlisle quarterback heaved a long pass without a Chicago defender anywhere near Exendine, who easily scored. Chicago's coach, the legendary Alonzo Stagg, protested profusely. However the score stood, given no rule outlawed the trick until the following year. The fabled Carlisle Indian School, led by Jim Thorpe,

The Committee considers as "confusing" the use of head protectors or jerseys (or attachments) which are so similar in color to the ball that they give the wearers an unfair and unsportsmanlike advantage over their opponents. If such head protectors are worn, the solid color must be broken by at least two cross stripes of a markedly contrasting color at least one inch in width and the solid color of jerseys (or attachments) must be definitely broken by stripes or numbers of markedly contrasting color.[37]

Equipment aside, another major change on the gridiron occurred in 1933. Although the *Spalding Guide* and NCAA commentary did not list the amendment among the most significant of the year, a new marking on the field of play was established. Rule 1 (The Field), Section 2, (Marking) was modified to include a new feature. In 1933, each five-yard stripe on the field was, for the first time, indicated at a right angle by short lines ten yards in from each of the sidelines. This was the advent of what became known as the "hash marks." The ball was to be moved between these hash marks for the commencement of all plays regardless of where the prior play ended.[38] All field markings were made with thoroughly slackened lime, for safety's sake. Officials were instructed not to allow games on fields marked with unslackened lime, given the danger of players suffering burns.

Hash marks were also part of the professional rules for the first time in 1933. A playoff game between the Chicago Bears and the Portsmouth Spartans for the 1932 NFL title (the teams ended the season tied for the top spot) was forced indoors by a waist-deep Chi-town snowfall. The playing surface began only two feet from the walls of the seating section. The teams agreed to bring the ball in from the sideline no less than fifteen feet on each play. The new style of play, favored by players and fans alike, gave birth to hash marks as a permanent feature of the

---

prevailed 18–4. The players' joy was heightened by outwitting the white boys. Anderson, *Carlisle vs. Army,* 163-164.

37 Okeson, *Spalding's Official Football Rules of the National Collegiate Athletic Association 1933,* 20.

38 Okeson, *Spalding's Official Football Rules of the National Collegiate Athletic Association 1933,* 3.

game.[39] One feature of the professional playing field was different from the college game. In the college game, the goal posts were located at the rear of the end zone, and not the goal line, as was the case in the professional version of the game. Not until 1974 were the NFL goal posts move to the end lines. While professional football adopted most of the intercollegiate rules, there were notable departures. The flying block and flying tackle were permitted in professional football. College restrictions on kickoff formations were not applicable in the NFL.[40] A professional player was not down until he was touched or tackled by an opponent when any portion of his body, except his hands or feet, was in contact with the ground.[41]

The passing game, only introduced in 1906, was still in metamorphosis during the 1930s. A professional player could pass the ball without penalty from any point behind the line of scrimmage in 1933. Such was not the case for his college counterpart. The collegiate passer had to be at least five yards behind the line of scrimmage. There were a number of other restrictions on passing that would be unfamiliar to the modern football fan.

Players on the ends of the line of scrimmage and players at least one yard behind the line were eligible to receive a pass; however, once an eligible receiver touched a pass, only that player was eligible to receive the pass. There were no tips or deflecting balls from one receiver to another in 1933. If the pass fell incomplete in the defense's end zone, the play resulted in a touchback and the opponents took possession on their twenty-yard line. A touchback for an incomplete pass in the end zone was eliminated in the professional game starting in 1933. A forward pass falling incomplete in the offense's end zone resulted in a safety. If a pass was touched by an originally ineligible player or by a player who became ineligible by going out of bounds, the penalty was loss of possession. The penalty could not be declined, though the team benefitting from the penalty could opt for a touchback if the foul occurred between their own ten-yard line and the goal. If a team made a second, third, or fourth incomplete pass, or illegal forward pass, in any series of downs, it would

39 Poule, *The Galloping Ghost, Red Grange*, 203.
40 http:/www.1920-30/sports/football.html.
41 Okeson, *Spalding's Official Football Rules of the National Collegiate Athletic Association 1933*, 34.

be penalized by five yards in addition to the loss of down. The five-yard penalty for incomplete passes was phased out of professional football at the end of the 1932 season, one of the improvements introduced by George Marshall to encourage scoring and excitement in the NFL. Rules regarding pass interference were substantially similar to modern rules. An intentionally grounded pass resulted in a loss of down and a fifteen-yard penalty which could not be declined. Lastly, a backward pass striking the ground or fumble recovered by the defenders could not be advanced.[42]

Football was a popular and successful game by 1933. The sport had attained a happy milepost in its development. There was no thought that improvements and change would not continue. The overseers of American football could justifiably marvel at the progress of their well-liked sport. With the passing of Edward Kimball Hall, it was a time to reflect. *Spalding's* editor Okeson noted:

> There is no feature in American collegiate foot ball, large or small, that does not reflect the genius of Edward K. Hall. In his long and stirring activities as a member of the Foot Ball Rules Committee he participated actively in the debates and discussions and in the confirmation or revisions of every clause in the code. Every game will be a final and lasting memorial of him. When the teams shift into their offensive formations, when the backs sweep in thrilling flight around the end, when the forward passes cut the air, the players will be executing the plays in a game which he largely contrived. When the stands and stadia resound with cheers and songs they will be enjoying custom, which he guided. Someone has said, "I care not who may write a country's laws provided I may write a country's songs." There is no comparison for him, however, who has created a country's greatest game. One by one, the brilliant beacons that illuminated the coast of foot ball in the pioneer past are flashing out. One by one, new

---

42 Okeson, *Spalding's Official Football Rules of the National Collegiate Athletic Association 1933,* 28-32.

games come into the chronicles of the sport. Yet, for us of the elder day, when games are coming to an end, and distant lights begin to twinkle in the twilight; for us, high over stands and scoreboards, against the background of the western sky, will burst into lines of flame the name of this great leader of American foot ball, this field marshal of American industry, this kindly, beloved companion—Edward Kimball Hall.[43]

---

43 Okeson, *Spalding's Official Football Rules of the National Collegiate Athletic Association 1933*, 15.

— *Chapter 4:* —

Professional Football's First Championship Game

> Marshall your adjectives. Bring out all the superlatives and shift them as you would juggle a jigsaw puzzle. All will fit in a description of a championship battle.
>
> —*Chicago Tribune,* December 18, 1933

The NFL recorded a momentous season in 1933. Not all the changes in the game were as regrettable as the prohibition on African-American participation. In fact, George Preston Marshall was responsible for some good in addition to shamefully drawing the curtain of racial segregation. Marshall, along with George Halas, helped usher in significant improvements to football. Marshall had one idea that would have a profound effect on the game. For the very first time, the NFL would decide its champion through a postseason game between the top teams of two newly formed divisions, East and West.[44]

Each division was comprised of five teams. NFL teams that competed in 1933 were as follows:

---

44 Oates, *The First 50 Years, The Story of The National Football League,* 220-221.

East	West
New York Giants	Chicago Bears
Brooklyn Dodgers	Portsmouth Spartans
Boston Redskins	Green Bay Packers
Philadelphia Eagles	Cincinnati Reds
Pittsburgh Pirates	Chicago Cardinals

The annual membership fee for a franchise in 1933 was ten thousand dollars.[45] The Pittsburgh Pirates were one of the league's new clubs.

Founded on July 8, 1933, by Arthur J. Rooney and A. McCool, the Pirates became the Pittsburgh Steelers in 1940. The Pirates had little success in 1933 and failed to win any championships during the organization's first four decades. When success finally came in the early 1970s, the football world rejoiced for Mr. Rooney, one of the NFL's oldest and most respected owners.

The Boston team was sporting a new name in 1933. The club had been established in Massachusetts' capital city the season before. Owner George Preston Marshall purchased franchise rights and inherited the players of the Newark Tornadoes, a team that failed and was sold back to the NFL. The club debuted as the Boston Braves, bearing the same name as the major-league baseball team that the football franchise shared a stadium with. The first season was not profitable and games were poorly attended. In 1933, the Braves became the Redskins and the team moved, sharing Fenway Park with the Red Sox.[46]

The Redskins' running back Jim Musick led the NFL in rushing in 1933. Musick, a native of Santa Ana, California, played college football for the University of Southern California Trojans. The 195-pound

---

45 http://www.profootballof.com/history/team.aspx?franchise_id 25 p1.

46 The Redskins' last season in Boston was 1936. Marshall moved the team to Washington DC in 1937. The last season in Boston was successful. The Redskins won the Eastern division championship. However, the next to the last game of the season at Fenway Park was so poorly attended that Marshall gave up a home field championship game, choosing to meet the Green Bay Packers at New York's Polo Grounds instead. The Redskins lost the game 21–6. http://www.sportsencyclopedia.com/NFL/wasbos/bosskins.html.

fullback was twenty-three years old during the 1933 season. Musick, who, characteristic of the age, played "both ways," also intercepted fourteen passes, good enough to rank third in the NFL that season.

Musick's teammate Cliff Battles, a tailback from Akron, Ohio, was the second leading rusher in the league during 1933.[47] Battles gained 737 yards, seventy-two yards less than Musick, although Battles had the NFL's highest yards per attempt at 5.4. Musick was second in the league with 4.7 yards per carry.

Despite the rushing prowess of the 1933 Redskins, the team posted a 5-5-2 record, good enough for only third place in the NFL's Eastern division. The final regular season standings for the season were as follows:

Team	W	L	T	W-L%	Pts	PtsA	PtDif
East							
New York Giants	11	3	0	.786	244	101	143
Brooklyn Dodgers	5	4	1	.556	93	54	39
Boston Redskins	5	5	2	.500	103	97	6
Philadelphia Eagles	3	5	1	.375	77	158	-81
Pittsburgh Pirates	3	6	2	.333	67	208	-141
West							
Chicago Bears	10	2	1	.833	133	82	51
Portsmouth Spartans	6	5	0	.545	128	87	41
Green Bay Packers	5	7	1	.417	170	107	63
Cincinnati Reds	3	6	1	.333	38	110	-72
Chicago Cardinals	1	9	1	.100	52	101	-49

The very first NFL championship game was played on December 17, 1933. The New York Giants, winner of the Eastern Division, traveled

47 Battles, a three-time first team All Pro, was inducted into the NFL Hall of Fame in 1968.

west to face the Western Division-leading Chicago Bears on the latter's home turf, Wrigley Field. The game was played before thirty thousand fans bundled against the cold. The historic contest featured NFL legend and Hall of Famer Bronislau "Bronko" Nagurski.

The discovery of Nagurski on a Minnesota farm is an entertaining part of football's folklore. As the tale has been told, Clarence "Fats" Spears, head coach of the University of Minnesota team, got lost in rural Minnesota. Nagurski, who was plowing a field without a horse, lifted his plow with one arm to point the awestruck coach in the right direction. Nagurski was signed to a full scholarship right then and there.

Born in Raining River, Ontario on November 3, 1908 to immigrants from the western Ukraine, Bronislau Nagurski got his famous nickname, "Bronko" from a teacher who could not pronounce his given name. The mispronunciation stuck and became one of football's most recognizable names. The Nagurskis moved from Canada to Minnesota while Bronko was a young boy.

Nagurski matured into a large and powerful man. At six foot two and 230 pounds, he played both defensive tackle and fullback for the University of Minnesota Gophers. Between 1927 and 1929, Nagurski helped lead the Gophers to an 18-4-2 record and a Big Ten championship in 1927. He was a consensus All-American tackle who was also named to a number of All-American teams as fullback—some voters named him for two positions.

Bronko Nagurski signed a professional football contract with the Chicago Bears in 1930. His professional career spanned from 1930 to 1937, as well as a comeback in 1943 when Nagurski and other former players were recalled to replace younger players who were in the service of the United States military during World War II.[48] His professional career was a thing of legend. The powerful fullback, one of the largest

---

48 Ronnie Cahill, one of only two Leominster High School graduates to play in the NFL, also played during 1943, his only professional season. Cahill, a standout at Leominster High School from 1931 to 1933, played across from Nagurski on the Bears' rival, the Chicago Cardinals. The other Leominster player who competed in the NFL was the legendary Lou Little, 1919-1921. Treat, *The Encyclopedia of Football: 16th Revised Edition*, 542.

of the time, was named to the NFL All Pro first team four times. He was elected to the NFL Hall of Fame in September 1963.

There are other Nagurski anecdotes. In 1934, New York Giants coach Steve Owen was in his team's locker room after a loss to the Bears. One of the sportswriters present queried, "Just how do you go about setting up a defense for a man like Bronko Nagurski?" The bewildered coach responded, "Defend him? There is only one way to defend Nagurski—shoot him before he leaves the dressing room."[49] Another story about the bruising fullback may not be rooted in reality; however, its repeated telling speaks, amusingly, about the perception of Bronko. Legend has it that during a scoring run against the Washington Redskins, he knocked two linebackers in opposite directions, ran over a defensive back and a safety, and bounced off the goal posts before slamming into Wrigley Field's brick wall. After the torturous trek, he returned to the huddle and was heard to say, "That last guy hit me awfully hard."[50]

Nagurski was at the height of his career during the 1933 and 1934 seasons. He was sixth in the NFL in all-purpose yards in 1934, with 586 yards rushing and 32 yards receiving. His 1933 all-purpose yards total (556) was good enough for fifth place in the league. Another Nagurski talent, passing, peaked in 1933 when the fullback threw for a career high 233 yards. By contrast, he notched a total of 474 yards through the air during the six years between 1932 and 1937. (Passing yardage records were not kept in 1930 and 1931). Bronko's arm would prove a valuable asset in the NFL's first championship game.

The talented Nagurski had another passion, one which outlasted his football career: professional wrestling. His professional football contract did not interfere with wrestling, even during the season.[51] During the summer of 1933, while most modern football players would be readying themselves for training camp, Nagurski was on the wrestling circuit. On July 18, 1933, the Bears fullback met Virginian Wee Willie Davis in a much-ballyhooed match at the Minneapolis Auditorium.

---

49 Hand, *Great Running Backs of the NFL*, 33.

50 *New York Times*, January 11, 1990.

51 During the 1937 football season, Nagurski played five football games with the Bears and wrestled in Duluth, Portland, Vancouver, Seattle, Phoenix, Los Angeles, Salt Lake City, and Intervall Falls. Hand, *Great Running Backs of the NFL*, 102-103.

Imagine a modern football coaching staff countenancing a player's involvement in the combat that follows:

> Davis aroused Narguski's ire early in the match by punching him on the chin with several lusty swings, the Bronko retaliating by flooring Wee Willie with a resounding smash to the jaw. This punch tamed Wee Willie for a time, but upon recovering he resumed his rough tactics with the result that spectators were treated to many thrilling moments from that time until Nagurski lifted his rival high in the air three times and crashed him to the canvas, the former football star leaping on Davis on his third trip to the mat and pinning his shoulders for the fall. Davis tried to attack Nagurski as the latter was leaving the ring, whereupon Bronko started back to resume the battle but a good old-fashioned rough and tumble fight was prevented by referee Shave with the assistance of several policemen.[52]

Bronko Nagurski wrestled until he was fifty-two years old, long after he left professional football. When he finally retired from wrestling in 1960, Nagurski's résumé included two world heavyweight championships and a variety of other titles. Nagurski was one of the most notable American athletes of the 1930s. One of his 1933 Bears' teammates was an icon of the prior decade.

Red Grange, as much as any player of his age, made professional football. Grange's professional football debut in 1925 was greatly anticipated. The former University of Illinois standout joined the Bears the night before Thanksgiving, immediately after the close of the college football season. Grange had an agent, Charles C. Pyle, whose initials were often said to stand for "Cold Cash Pyle." Pyle made a deal with Bears owner Halas: Grange would receive half of the money the team would make in what remained of the regular season as well as a number of exhibition games that were added to display Grange to eager fans.[53]

---

52 *Evening Tribune*, Alberta, Minnesota, July 19, 1933. The sportswriter's use of the adjective "former" football star is a bit curious given Nagurski was at the peak of his football playing days.

53 Hand, *Great Running Backs of the NFL*, 50.

Pyle got half of Grange's cut. The Bears scheduled a total of ten games in eighteen days. One of those games rescued the failing New York Giants and their owner Tim Mara.[54] The Polo Grounds packed in seventy thousand fans to watch the Giants host the Bears and Grange. Some of the fans paid three or four times face value of their tickets. Grange's take from the game was an astounding thirty thousand dollars. By 1933, "the Galloping Ghost" was near the end of his career, which ended in 1934. The 1920s belonged to Red Grange, Babe Ruth, Jack Dempsey, and Bobby Jones. The exuberant decade had changed American sports. The first NFL championship game would feature first-rate talents, one each from the first two decades of the NFL. The older man called Nagurski the greatest player he had ever seen as the Bears prepared to face the Giants in the first NFL title clash.

That first championship contest lived up to its promise. The game, featuring no less than eight future Hall of Fame players, was an exciting, closely played contest with six lead changes.[55] The Bears held the early lead thanks to two field goals by Jack Manders. The Giants responded with the first touchdown in NFL championship game history. On the strength of a twenty-nine-yard pass from Morris "Red" Badgro to Harry Newman, and a successful try after, the Giants took the lead 7–6.

The game stayed close throughout the second half. The Bears retook the lead on a fifteen-yard Jack Manders field goal, his third of the game. The third lead change came when the Giants put together a drive that was punctuated by a Mat Krause one-yard touchdown plunge. The Giants' 14–9 lead did not last long. Nagurski helped spark his team with both his legs and arm. The Bears fullback gained sixty-five yards on the ground, a sizable accumulation for the age, especially when considering that the league leader, Jim Musick, gained 809 total yards over twelve games.

---

54 Mara, the bookie owner of the Giants, had frantically tried to sign Grange earlier that year on a trip west. His nine-year-old son Wellington prayed that Dad would sign his idol. Poole, *The Galloping Ghost*, 131.

55 In addition to players Red Grange, Bill Hewitt, William "Link" Lyman, George Musso, and Bronko Nagurski for the Bears and Morris "Red" Badgro, Ray Flaherty, Mel Hein, and Ken Strong for the Giants, Chicago owner/coach George Halas, Giants coach Steve Owen, and Giants owner Tim Mara were all future Hall of Famers. http://www.profootballhof. com.

Nagurski's passing prowess proved just as important. He executed an eight-yard scoring pass to end Bill Kerr in the third quarter, putting the Windy City team ahead 16–14. The Giants engineered their own eight-yard touchdown on a pass from Ken Strong to Newman. The Giants retook the lead on the game's fifth lead change. The score was now 21–16 New York. But Nagurski would answer the call once more.

The game was in its closing minutes. Nagurski took the ball and broke toward the line of scrimmage. The Giants defense had to honor the bruising fullback's running threat. As the defense drew in, Nagurski suddenly stopped, leaped in the air and rifled a fourteen-yard pass to fellow future Hall of Famer Bill Hewitt, who, as per his custom, was playing without a helmet. Hewitt quickly lateralled the ball to Bill Kerr who raced into the end zone. The sixth and final lead change cemented the Bears' 23–21 victory, but not without some last-second drama. With the clock ticking down to the final whistle, the Giants' Dale Burnett caught a pass and started down the sideline. The streaking Burnett tried to lateral, hoping to pull off a stunning final touchdown. Red Grange, playing at defensive back, stopped Burnett, trapping the ball and pinning Burnett's arms, which prevented the intended lateral to a runner trailing the play. The saving tackle was the game's last play. Halas said it was the smartest play that he had ever seen. Grange's contribution made for a poetic ending to a truly memorable game.

Each member of the winning team earned $210.34. The Giants' per-player take was $140.22.[56] The inaugural NFL championship game had all the ingredients vital to the future of professional football. Established legends and new stars competed on a grand stage in the most dramatic of fashions. The sport was still developing in popularity, but 1933 signaled a turning point. In a year that Americans weathered uncertainty and despair, football was a staple that provided some relief. In the midst of hard times, football not only persevered but enhanced its appeal. Like America itself, football was resilient. That irrepressible, rough hewn spirit qualified football as a uniquely American game.

---

56 Each members of the winning team in Super Bowl XLIV earned $83,000, the losers each took home $42,000. NFL Collective Bargaining Agreement 2006-2012, Article XLII; Post Season Pay, 194.

— *Chapter 5:* —

Convincing Starts

With pulses beating a little faster, with crisp autumnal air a little frostier and with spirits a little jauntier, hundreds of the faithful will turnout at Doyle Field to see Leominster High School inaugurate the 1933 gridiron campaign.

—*Bill Yeaw,*
Leominster Enterprise,
September 22, 1933

During the first days of September, coaches for Leominster and Fitchburg went about the business of readying their charges for the fall season. Coach Clarence Amiott of the Fitchburg team attended a football program at Northwestern University in August. Amiott was eager to share the innovations learned there with his players. Coach Handley of the host school and coach Jones of USC provided first-rate coaching clinics which the Fitchburg coach enthusiastically attended.[57]

Fitchburg's hopes for the 1933 season were high. One hundred young men turned out for the football team. The Red and Gray fielded a veteran squad. Every starter from the 1932 team returned with the

---

57 *Leominster Enterprise*, September 11, 1933.

exception of the center position. The Esielionis brothers, Stanley and Felix, stars of Fitchburg's 1932 team, were named co-captains of the 1933 edition. Fitchburg was strengthened by the addition of halfback Bill Mackie. Mackie transferred to Fitchburg High School for his senior year. His prior three high school seasons were spent leading the team at St. Bernard's, a Catholic school located in Fitchburg. The six-foot-three southpaw pitcher and first baseman played in a summer baseball league. During the summer of 1933, Mackie's athleticism on the baseball field caught the attention of two Fitchburg businessmen. Bucky Richards, the manager of Flynn Towel, a towel and linen supplier, and Johnny Morin, the manager of the Hotel Raymond, wanted Mackie to bring his talents to the public high school. The men were successful in convincing the gifted athlete to enroll at Fitchburg High School for the fall term. Fitchburg fans soon learned what Richards and Morin already knew.

The Red and Gray were looking to improve in 1933. Fitchburg had posted a disappointing 4-4-2 mark the prior season. One of the losses was to a powerful Leominster team on Thanksgiving. The Blue and White beat Fitchburg 25–0 in the holiday classic, the second-largest winning margin by a Leominster team since the teams began their rivalry in 1894. The undefeated Leominster team outscored their opponents 205–12 in 1932.[58]

Leominster's expectations for 1933 were guarded. Eighty-five candidates showed up for the football team, but all of the prior season's starters except one were lost to graduation. Ronnie Cahill, a triple threat with astonishing talent as a runner, passer, and kicker, was the player Leominster looked to for its success in the new campaign. The enrollment at Fitchburg High School was more than double that of Leominster. The Red and Gray had a much larger pool from which to recruit talent. Leominster's Warriors had their work cut out for them.

While teams in both cities opened their practice sessions with calisthenics, grass drills, and tackling dummies, the nation and the new president were coping with unprecedented economic difficulties. During August and September, local newspapers monitored support for the National Recovery Administration (NRA). The NRA was charged with enforcement of codes that established fair practices concerning working conditions, wages, and business activity. Companies that

---

58 *Fitchburg Sentinel*, November 22, 1932.

complied with the NRA displayed the emblematic Blue Eagle in their windows. Organizers divided Leominster into eight districts each with a captain assigned to oversee canvassers. The latter went door to door with pledge cards asking citizens from all walks of life to give their support to the NRA. Lamothe Hall, on Leominster's Third Street, hosted the city's largest NRA rally when 650 people attended a meeting moderated by Col. J. Henry Goguen. Leominster Mayor Platt spoke, exhorting the attendees to help revive the economy with patriotic exercise of purchasing power. If a product was needed, he advised, "don't delay … buy it now."[59]

Fifty percent of the city's voters had pledged compliance with the NRA by September 1. They did not reach the lofty goal of 100 percent adherence. The campaign did succeed in signing up two-thirds of city voters before the first week of September came to a close.[60]

Schools opened in Leominster and Fitchburg on Wednesday, September 6. The 185 high school boys engaged in football practice sessions on behalf of each high school were nearly matched by 180 young men at work in the Leominster State Forest on behalf of the Civilian Conservation Corporation (CCC). Earning between $30 and $45 per month, the workers age eighteen to thirty camped in the woods where they worked.[61] Another organization grouped within President Roosevelt's New Deal, the CCC was formed to adopt a variety of conservation measures, which included clearing dead wood, drainage improvements, and tree planting. The young men who headed out to football practice must have felt a certain degree of privilege when considering the arduous labor that faced CCC crews.

The high schools announced their schedules for the 1933 season on Thursday, September 12. Leominster's football schedule for 1933 was as follows:

9/23	Quincy	Home
9/30	Athol	Home
10/7	Amesbury	Home
10/12	Chelsea	Home

---

59 *Leominster Enterprise*, August 30, 1933.
60 *Leominster Enterprise*, September 5, 1933.
61 *Leominster Enterprise*, September 6, 1933.

10/21	Rogers	Away
10/28	Framingham	Away
11/11	Gardner	Away
11/14	Clinton	Home
11/18	Andover	Home
11/30	Fitchburg	Home

Fitchburg's slate of games featured as much geographic diversity as Leominster's. Both faced opponents from larger cities with significantly higher school enrollments. There were plenty of challenges. The Red and Gray "Chargers," as they were nicknamed in those days, faced the following schools:

9/23	Keene, NH	Home
9/30	Lynn General Electric	Home
10/7	Providence Central	Home
10/14	Arlington	Home
10/21	Framingham	Home
10/28	Gardner	Home
11/4	Brookline	Home
11/11	Brockton	Away
11/18	Quincy	Home
11/25	Chicopee	Home
11/30	Leominster	Away

Amiott was able to arrange an eleven-game schedule for Fitchburg that included only two away games, one of which was the short trip to neighboring Leominster on Thanksgiving Day.

Before the holiday classic at Doyle Field on the last day of November, the teams had more than two months of football to play. Practices during the weeks before opening the season were hampered by a hurricane battering the east coast. The storm made landfall on September 15 on the Outer Banks of North Carolina. More than twenty people lost their lives; damage was also substantial in New England. Nearly seven inches of rain fell on Fitchburg and Leominster by September 18. Like the storm raging outdoors, Leominster boxer Tony Celli ravaged his noteworthy Boston opponent "KO" Kasper. Local fans jammed into the auditorium of Leominster's City Hall on the evening of September 16 to watch the bout. Celli punctuated Kasper's nickname, but not in the way his opponent planned, when he knocked out Kasper in the second round.[62] One week later, Leominster and Fitchburg readied for their respective first tests on the gridiron.

For their opener, Leominster hosted the Granite City football eleven of Quincy High School. Quincy was predicted to be a big hurdle for the Blue and White Warriors. Local sportswriter Bill Yeaw wrote, "Leominster will clearly have to resort to an open, overhead brand of football to pull the chestnuts out of the fire."[63] Leominster coach Charlie Broderick may have been a bit more confident. Sophomore Americo Spacciapoli sat quietly in the locker room prior to the initial game of his first high school football season. The coach had his full attention. The Boston newspapers had previewed the game. Broderick snapped, "Quincy at Leominster, not worth the drive." The print media of Massachusetts' capital city had determined Quincy's dominance before a single play was executed. The coach continued, "How can anyone look into your heart and determine what you have inside?" [64] The Leominster players were ready to play their own game of football.

Quincy was vanquished from start to finish. Leominster thoroughly dominated the visitors from the eastern part of the state. The *Leominster Enterprise* recorded the thrashing:

> Leominster High School's Blue and White Warriors opened the season auspiciously Saturday afternoon at Doyle Field by running amuck over heavier, slower foes from Quincy, scoring an overwhelming 46–0 victory. With an attack of speed, versatility, and power that was pregnant with great possibility, the Broderick coached eleven proceeded to give their beefier, but more sodden opponents a lesson on the clarifications of modern football a la Rockne, and in the end the result was a surprising waterloo to the high hopes of Quincy.[65]

---

62 *Leominster Enterprise*, September 18, 1933.
63 *Leominster Enterprise*, September 19, 1933.
64 Celli and Piermarini, *The Rivalry*, DVD.
65 *Leominster Enterprise*, September 25, 1933.

Led by the multi-talented Ronnie Cahill, Leominster piled up yards and points, besting Quincy in every aspect of the game. The visitors were shocked. So great was their dismay that Quincy formed a committee to "investigate" the game. When word got out, the committee members backed away from the "investigation" label and downplayed the whole exercise as a "review." By the time Leominster played its second game against Athol, the *Enterprise* was calling Quincy the "City of Presidents and Investigations." Quincy representatives were in attendance at Doyle Field for the Athol contest "to see why a Leominster team should be able to beat Quincy." The curious contingent that visited what was most certainly viewed as rural Massachusetts "were surprised to see that there was such a team in these parts."[66] The committee came away with not only an appreciation for Leominster football, but also for the fine football stadium. Doyle Field was one of the finest football venues in the state, and the Quincy supporters recognized that their field did not compare to Leominster's palace.[67]

Fitchburg also had a fabled football stadium, Crocker Field. The gift of local business magnate and philanthropist Alvah Crocker, the field was opened in June 1918. Legend has it that Babe Ruth visited Fitchburg in 1920 and had an opportunity to view the field. The Red Sox slugger asked what college played there. He was incredulous that the stadium was home to a high school team. Crocker Field's designers, the Olmstead brothers, were prominent architects who were responsible for landscape designs at Harvard Business School, the University of Notre Dame, the University of Chicago, and Vassar College. Babe Ruth's disbelief was understandable.

Fitchburg's first opponent in 1933, like Leominster's, had to travel. Fitchburg hosted Keene High School from southwestern New Hampshire. Fitchburg didn't know exactly what to expect from the New Hampshire boys, but the Red and Gray approached the game with confidence. Once play began, "Keene was much stronger than the fans and probably Fitchburg High expected and for three periods offered stubborn, dogged resistance."[68]

---

66 *Leominster Enterprise*, October 3, 1933.
67 *Leominster Enterprise*, October 3, 1933.
68 *Fitchburg Sentinel*, September 25, 1933.

After three complete quarters of play, the score stood at Fitchburg 6, Keene 0. The host team had managed the lone score during a first-period drive that featured the running of right halfback Bill Mackie. Mackie gained fifty-five yards on two carries which established the ball on Keene's five-yard line. Fitchburg made three attempts to score, two of which were Mackie runs that netted only a single yard. On fourth down, Mackie burst through the line for Fitchburg's touchdown.

New recruit Mackie was paying immediate dividends. The game finally opened up in the fourth quarter. The home team, through a skillful use of reserves, wore down their opponents. Mackie left the game early in the second quarter when he suffered a lacerated lip. Under the rules of the day, a player who left the game could not return to play during the quarter he left the game. The team physician walked Mackie a few blocks to his Academy Street office where he sutured the halfback's lip. Mackie returned to the game in the third quarter.[69] He advanced the ball thirty-eight yards on two running plays, once again providing his team a scoring opportunity from the Keene five-yard line. This time it took Mackie three attempts to cross the goal line for the Red and Gray's second score. Mackie kicked the extra point and Fitchburg led 13–0.

On Fitchburg's next possession, halfback Kallagher tossed two long passes to backfield mate Mackie, the first thirty-five yards from midfield to the Keene fifteen. On the next play Kallagher connected with Mackie in the end zone for Fitchburg's third and final touchdown. The home team earned a hard-fought, solid 19–0 victory.

The contributions of Bill Mackie on behalf of Fitchburg and Ronnie Cahill for Leominster were noteworthy. Each city was content to have inaugurated the 1933 season with big wins. Everywhere the mood was hopeful, though even the most zealous rooters knew that each team faced daunting challengers in the weeks ahead.

---

69 Interview with Bill Mackie, November 19, 2009. His helmet was outfit-ted with a facemask, a rarity at the time. Mackie wore the facemask, at his coach's insistence, for the remainder of the season.

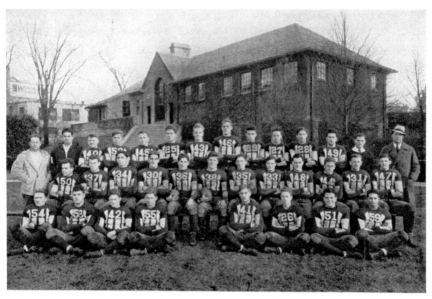

The 1933 Fitchburg High School team pictured in front of the Crocker Field House.

The Leominster High School team of 1933 built on the success of the prior year's undefeated squad.

A collector's pin celebrating the success of the 1933 Leominster High School football team.

The legendary Ronnie Cahill, who was a triple threat at Leominster High School from 1931 to 1933. Cahill starred at Holy Cross and played one season for the Chicago Cardinals of the NFL in 1943.

William Bernard Mackie

Football, Basketball '34

*His limbs are cut in manly
mould,
For hardy sports and contest
bold.*

Bill's ever smiling face and care-free nature, along with his out-standing athletic ability have made him an idol of many. Although, Bill isn't so very keen on studying, we trust that he will make the grade.

Bill Mackie's 1934 Fitchburg High School yearbook photo. Mackie played for the school for only the 1933 season.

Ed Sullivan, captain of the 1929 Fitchburg High School football team, escorted Bill Mackie to Crocker Field on Thanksgiving Day 1933 where the team bus waited for the ride to Leominster's Doyle Field.

AIRPLANE VIEW OF DOYLE FIELD

ſouvenír
FOOTBALL PROGRAM
FITCHBURG at LEOMINSTER
Thanksgiving Day
1 9 3 3

10 cents

The 1933 Thanksgiving program described a battle of undefeated teams from Fitchburg and Leominster.

Coach Amiott Says . . .

Football is one of the most popular out-of-door games that we know of today. It teaches the value of a sound body, the spirit of co-operation and fair play to those that take an active part in it. It takes strong, healthy bodies to play football.

Vitamin D is the best known substance for the building of stronger bones and healthier teeth. Incorporating Vitamin D in bread is a step in the direction of better health.

Coach C. N. Amiott

Coach Broderick Says . . .

There has been much talk against football in relation to health. I believe that football is a fine type of a game which tends to develop and build stronger, healthier, and better fitted men for the life that is ahead of them when school days are over.

There has been a movement toward vitaminizing certain foods which form staple articles of diet for young and old, which also will build better health. Chiefly among these is the incorporation of Vitamin D in bread. It is a fine movement.

Coach Charles B. Broderick

TOWN TALK VITAMIN D BREAD

for stronger bones and healthier teeth

SWANSON BAKING CO.

The back cover of the 1933 Leominster-Fitchburg game program, picturing the legendary head coach of each team.

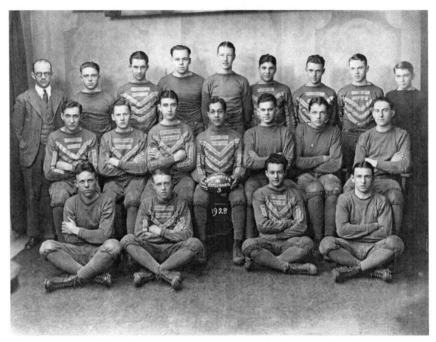

The 1928 Leominster High School football team was led by a player of African-American descent. Captain Charlie Hazard holds the football.

Legendary Columbia University coach and Leominster native Lou Little led his team to one of college football's greatest upsets when Columbia defeated Stanford 7–0 in the 1934 Rose Bowl.

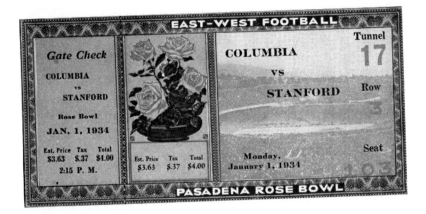

A ticket to the 1934 Rose Bowl game between Stanford and Columbia.

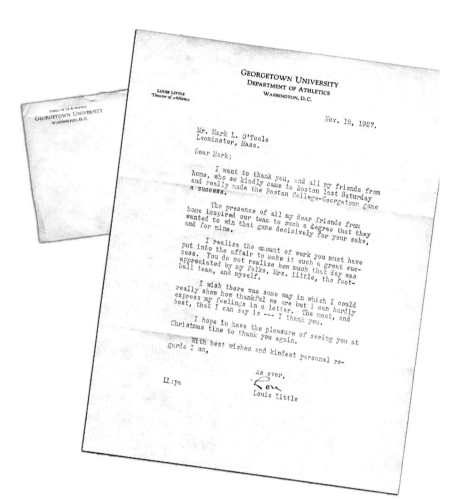

GEORGETOWN UNIVERSITY
DEPARTMENT OF ATHLETICS
WASHINGTON, D.C.

LOUIS LITTLE
Director of Athletics

Nov. 18, 1927.

Mr. Mark L. O'Toole
Leominster, Mass.

Dear Mark;

I want to thank you, and all my friends from home, who so kindly came to Boston last Saturday and really made the Boston College-Georgetown game a success.

The presence of all my dear friends from home inspired our team to such a degree that they wanted to win that game decisively for your sake, and for mine.

I realize the amount of work you must have put into the affair to make it such a great success. You do not realize how much that day was appreciated by my folks, Mrs. Little, the football team, and myself.

I wish there was some way in which I could really show how thankful we are but I can hardly express my feelings in a letter. The most, and best, that I can say is --- I thank you.

I hope to have the pleasure of seeing you at Christmas time to thank you again.

With best wishes and kindest personal regards I am,

As ever,

Lou

Louis Little

LL:pa

A letter from Lou Little to his friend Mark O'Toole thanking him for attending Georgetown's game against Boston College. O'Toole played in the very first Leominster-Fitchburg game on October 20, 1894.

President Franklin Roosevelt tours in an open car with Herbert Hoover during his inauguration March 4, 1933. The open car is similar to the one Roosevelt occupied in Miami when he dodged an assassination attempt on February 15, 1933.

Future President Franklin Roosevelt in 1913, the year he was appointed assistant secretary of the Navy—eight years before he was crippled by polio.

Crime fighter J. Edgar Hoover, whose government career stretched from 1921 to 1972. Hoover reinvigorated federal law enforcement in 1933, resulting in the capture of several notorious gangsters the following year.

A postal cover commemorating the Century of Progress exhibition which opened in Chicago during 1933 with hopes that a display of modern technology would help stimulate the ailing American economy.

Public enemy number one John Dillinger, who menaced America during 1933.

Breadlines were an all-too-common sight in America during the Great Depression.

Isador Lubin, commissioner of labor and statistics in the Roosevelt Administration, stands by a graph showing the rise in production of consumer goods during the three years subsequent to 1933, the depth of the Great Depression.

A young boy receives soup from a relief mission.

Harold "Red" Grange, whose entry into the NFL during 1925 helped popularize the professional game.

Bronislau "Bronko" Nagurski, signed by the Chicago Bears, was one of the most rugged players of his day. He lead the Bears to victory in the NFL's first championship game on December 17, 1933.

The Redskins go through an unusual practice routine during their first season in Washington DC. The team started in Boston during 1932 but moved to Washington after the 1936 season.

Redskins' owner George Marshall (left), who made critical changes to the NFL, including infamously segregating professional football, is pictured with his head coach Ray Flaherty during the team's first season in Washington.

President-elect Calvin Coolidge on the way to his inauguration. Before Chicago Bears owner George Halas and his new star Red Grange visited the White House in 1925, Coolidge thought the Bears were an animal act.

A student sketch from the 1934 Fitchburg High School yearbook, *The Boulder,* depicts the importance of the 1933 football season.

The Esielionis brothers, Felix (left) and Stanley, were Fitchburg High School's 1933 co-captains. Together they anchored the Fitchburg line, Felix at left guard and Stanley at left tackle.

The 1933-34 Fitchburg High School marching band entertained fans during the football season.

Early football action from Crocker Field, Fitchburg.

The talents of Fitchburg's Bill Mackie are depicted in this 1933 sketch.

Danny Bell played quarterback, fullback, and defensive back for Leominster High School in 1933.

A young Joe Goodhue developed a resourcefulness and work ethic in the 1920s that would serve him well during the difficult years of the Great Depression.

Ronnie Cahill poses as a member of the NFL's Chicago Cardinals in 1943.

Ronnie Cahill poses during his 1937-1939 playing days at Holy Cross.

Ronnie Cahill as player for U.S. Navy Pre-Flight School during World War II. Official U.S. Navy photograph.

Two youthful players get caught up in popularity of football during the mid-1930s.

— Chapter 6: —

College Football and the Great Depression

Lou Little was upset. He felt betrayed. In late October 1929, virtually coincidental with the market crash, the Carnegie Foundation released a report on the state of college football. The study was a broad indictment of a system that featured widespread financial inducement in recruiting and retaining players during an age when any benefits afforded players were viewed as antithetical to what amateur athletics stood for. Little was a football coach with an impeccable reputation. The mention of his program in the report was unwarranted and underhanded.

Little, a Leominster native, was Georgetown University's football coach and athletic director from 1924 to 1929. An investigator from the Carnegie Foundation visited Georgetown in the fall of 1927. According to Little, Carnegie's John T. McGovern had given Little assurances that nothing was deemed to be amiss at Georgetown. Little offered to back up his statement with a letter written by McGovern at the time of his visit to Georgetown. The investigator had confirmed his oral assertions to Little: athletics at Georgetown were in compliance with amateur standards.

Little's reaction to the report was echoed by coaches and college athletic administrators throughout the nation. Criticism ranged from direct questioning of the findings to suggestions that the authors had sensationalized the state of affairs through generalizations and innuendo.

Ultimately, the worsening economy had more of an impact on college football than the Carnegie findings. The Great Depression reduced game attendance significantly. Some estimates indicate that crowds had fallen off by 25 percent.[70] Alumni could neither afford to attend games nor fund subsidies at the same pace as before the Depression. In some ways, the nation's financial woes postponed reform of college football.

The Depression also impacted the safety of the game. Less money meant fewer coaches with less training, and insufficient equipment. Smaller colleges and high schools were particularly hard-hit. Sparse training, especially at the high-school level, produced an unprecedented number of deaths throughout the 1930s. Most deaths resulted from head and neck injuries, though heat stroke was often to blame. While there were a number of deaths in college football during the 1930s, including eight in 1931, the numbers did not rival 1905 when nineteen college players died on the gridiron.[71] In a very fortunate anomaly, no deaths were recorded in the college game during 1933.[72]

College football hit its financial nadir in 1933. Attendance was at an all-time low. Gate receipts did not rebound until the middle of the decade. College football began to rebound in 1935, beginning with larger crowds. Programs competed for a share of the increasing revenues. With renewed vigor, schools honed their systems of recruitment and player subsidies. Some schools attempted to enhance revenues with commercial radio broadcast contracts. Cities struggled to create economic growth and looked to Pasadena's Rose Bowl, which originated in 1902, as a model. In 1933 it was college football's only postseason bowl.[73] That year represented a point of demarcation. It was an important year for the nation and for college football.

---

70 Watterson, *College Football*, 177.

71 Okeson, *Spalding's Official Football Rules of the National Collegiate Athletic Association 1933,* 18-19.

72 Watterson, *College Football*, 181.

73 1935 brought the Orange Bowl to Miami and the Sugar Bowl to New Orleans. The Cotton Bowl was established in Dallas two years later.

In 1933, Lou Little was the head coach of Columbia University's football team. Little was hired by Columbia in 1930. The sixty-eight-thousand-dollar salary offered by the Ivy League school could not be matched by Georgetown. The coach had great success during his days coaching the Hoyas. In 1927, Georgetown posted a 9-1 record with Little at the helm. The one loss came at the hands of Syracuse University by a score of 19–6. The nine victories included wins over prominent football schools including West Virginia, Lafayette, and Boston College. Even more remarkable, Georgetown only surrendered a total of two points in those wins.

The success Little enjoyed at Georgetown followed him to Columbia. Little's fourth season at the helm of Columbia proved to be a memorable one. The 1933 Columbia football campaign started with great promise. The coach was eager to build on the team's success of the prior year. Columbia prevailed in the first seven games of the 1932 season, including a 7–6 victory over Navy. Their last two contests did not result in wins. Columbia lost in its next to last game to Brown, 7–6, and ended its season in a scoreless tie with Syracuse. By any reasonable measure, the year had been a success. The future was bright, with talented signal caller Clifford Montgomery returning for the 1933 season.[74]

The Lions opened their 1933 season with wins over Lehigh, 39–0, and Virginia, 15–6. The team's third game was against the Princeton Tigers. The Lions were beaten 20–0. Princeton went on to post an undefeated season. Columbia recovered quickly from the loss.

The talented young men from Manhattan's northern end reeled off five consecutive victories to close out their regular season. The Lions defeated:

Penn State	33–0
Cornell	9–6
Navy	14–7
Lafayette	46–6
Syracuse	16–0

---

74 Okeson, *Spalding's Official Football Rules of the National Collegiate Athletic Association 1933* , 23-25

Columbia's accomplishments on the gridiron began to garner national attention. Since most of New York's sportswriters were nationally syndicated, the university's location helped spread the word of their success across the country. When the Lions beat Navy it did not escape notice that the Midshipmen had shutout perennial power Notre Dame by a score of 7–0 just the week before. The Lions were developing a following. The school did not enjoy the reputation or respect of some larger football programs; however, a sense did prevail that something special was developing in Morningside Heights.

By season's end, polls established undefeated Michigan as the unofficial national champion. The second-ranked team in the nation was Stanford. The Stanford Indians had a record of 8-1-1. Stanford lost to Washington State 6–0 and played Northwestern to a scoreless tie. An all-important win came at the expense of USC. When Stanford met USC on November 11, 1933, the Trojans had not suffered a defeat in twenty-six games. During the previous season, USC had beaten Stanford on its way to an undefeated mark, which included a Rose Bowl victory over Pittsburgh, 35–0, and a national championship. The 1932 loss prompted the Stanford class of 1936 to vow never to lose to USC again. The press caught wind of the pledge and the Stanford gridders became known as the "Vow Boys." True to their word, the Indians defeated the Trojans in 1933 by a score of 13–7.

The victory over USC earned Stanford the Pacific Coast championship. During those days, tradition permitted the Pacific Coast champion to choose its own Rose Bowl opponent. Until the advent of the Orange Bowl and Sugar Bowl in 1935, Pasadena's Rose Bowl was the only game in town as far as postseason competition went. Stanford, which had defeated all of its West Coast rivals, including the mighty Trojans, could not find any takers for an invitation to the Rose Bowl.

Stanford sought the strongest of opponents for the season's pinnacle and tendered offers to both the Princeton Tigers and the Wolverines of Michigan. The undefeated Tigers declined. So did Michigan, the unofficial national champion. The Michigan roster included future president Gerald Ford, a back-up center.[75] Stanford's next invitee was

---

75 Gerald Ford started at center for Michigan in 1934, however, the Michigan Wolverines suffered a reversal of fortune posting only a 1-7 record

the darling of the New York City press and a team that recorded a convincing win in its last game of the season.

The Columbia Lions had enchanted the Gotham City's newspaper columnists. Momentum grew as their victories mounted. When the Lions defeated powerful Syracuse in the season's finale by a score of 16–0, the news traveled throughout the nation. Stanford made the offer: Columbia was invited to travel across America and play in the historic Rose Bowl game.

The offer created a good deal of controversy. The notion of an Ivy League school, a bastion of academics, participating in big-time college football seemed odd. Debate stirred. The administration feared tarnishing the school's image as well as risking a potential embarrassment on the gridiron. Football odds makers were predicting a Stanford rout, some by as many as sixty points. At the urging of Little and alumni, Columbia's dean was persuaded to accept Stanford's invitation.[76]

The decision was not without its critics. The school's daily newspaper, the *Spectator*, commented, "The Lion has joined the circus." The paper editorialized further:

> Columbia must bear the charge of overemphasizing intercollegiate football. The squad has just completed one of the most successful seasons in Morningside history. Now the team is to be sent 3,000 miles away to show its unique ability in booting a tiny pigskin before mobs for whom this university signifies solely a good football team.
>
> In taking this action, Columbia must be accused of deliberate disregard of those statements which its own athletic investigating committee made last February:
>
> "… however, that these contests ought not to be conducted as public spectacle for profit. We should look forward with such pleasure to reorganization of athletics as would confine to members to the university and their

---

that season, the inverse of 1933. http://bentley.umich.edu/athdept/football/fbteam/1934/.

76 http://www.gocolumbialions.com, 75 Years Ago Columbia Wins Rose Bowl.

alumni …" The men who accepted this invitation will not deny that the game is a tremendous money-making proposition no matter how much will be distributed to charities …

The editorial expression is not an attack upon the men who compose the varsity squad. We realize fully what a thrill it is to them to be singled out as gridiron representatives of the East. The men themselves are as clean a group of players and gentlemen as any college can boast about. But is not a question of personalities so much as it is a question of principles.[77]

Despite the criticism, charges of profits taking precedence over academics, and the dire predictions of football experts, the Columbia Lions made their way across the nation. When their train finally arrived in California, the New Yorkers were greeted by rains that soaked the region and the field for nearly a week prior to the game. The conditions were so bad that some thought was given to postponing the contest.[78]

The muddy field, which had to be repaired before the game could proceed, may have slowed the mighty Stanford offense some, but not entirely. Bobby Grayson, the Indians' talented running back, still managed 100 yards on the ground, a rarity for the era. The game was played in a heavy rain, the worst precipitation since 1879.[79] Stanford made a number of deep incursions into Columbia territory, but each was repulsed by a strong Lions' defense, penalties, or fumbles.

Columbia had its chances as well. A first-quarter drive deep into Stanford's side was halted on the fifteen-yard line. Al Barabas fumbled and Stanford recovered. Another first-period Columbia drive faltered on the Stanford two-yard line when quarterback Cliff Montgomery lost a fumble of his own.

The second period brought the Lions another scoring opportunity. Montgomery dropped back to pass as end Tony Matal broke down the field. Stanford star Grayson matched Matal step for step in coverage.

---

77 *Barnard Bulletin*, Ed. Gertrude Epstein. Columbia U. Vol. 38, December 8, 1933, No. 17, 3–4.
78 http://www.50columbians.com, 75 Years Ago: Columbia Wins Rose Bowl!
79 *San Mateo Times*, January 2, 1934.

Montgomery heaved the ball. The crowd of thirty-five thousand collectively held its breath. Matal, also known as "Mad Anthony," brought the ball into his chest to complete a twenty-three-yard reception.[80] The Lions were set up on Stanford's seventeen.

Little signaled the Lions' next play. Montgomery got his orders—KF 79 was the play. The talented quarterback took the snap and motioned a handoff to halfback Ed Brominski. Brominski and all the Lions' charging interference thrust to the right. Montgomery pulled the ball back. It was a deft fake. Without Stanford's defenders noticing, Montgomery handed the ball to fullback Barabas who sprinted to the left, "naked" of any blockers and without detection. Barabas coursed the seventeen yards untouched. Columbia was on the board with the first score of the game. The Lions converted the try after and the score stood 7–0.[81]

The second half of the game saw the Columbia defense tested on a number of drives. The Lions were challenged no less than three times in the third period alone. The first attack ended when a fifteen-yard penalty killed a Stanford drive that had advanced to the Columbia twenty-yard line. Two more Stanford drives failed as a result of fumbles. Stanford turned the ball over to the Lions on the Columbia thirteen-yard line and later on the Columbia one. After three quarters, the score remained Columbia 7, Stanford 0.[82]

One quarter of rain-soaked football remained. The Stanford fans were gravely concerned. What seemed unthinkable only a few hours before was clearly in the realm of possibility. Stanford mounted a furious drive.

Columbia dressed only seventeen players but their men were well-rested. The underdogs from the east took everything Stanford could throw at them. The bench, as meager as it was, proved an important part of the game. Al Ciampa ("pronounced 'Champa' in the quaint Italian way," according to *Los Angeles Times* columnist Bill Henry) shored up the Lions' line and stopped a number of runs including some of Grayson's hard charges. Henry's post-game story noted, "whenever President Roosevelt needs someone to plug a leak in the budget I'd like

---

80 *Oakland Sports Tribune,* January 2, 1934.
81 *San Mateo Times,* January 2, 1934.
82 *San Mateo Times,* January 2, 1934.

to recommend Ciampa, who replaced Wilder backing up the left side of Columbia's line. Ciampa promptly took charge and low!"[83]

The Lions' defense exhausted Stanford. The Indians' last drive was stopped on the Columbia two-yard line, turning the ball over on downs. Despite being outgained on offense by Stanford 334 to 148, Columbia had traveled west and won. It was the first time since Harvard defeated Oregon by a score of 7–6 in 1920 that an eastern team had claimed victory at the Rose Bowl. The Columbia Lions had accomplished an upset of epic proportions.[84]

Weeks of accolades and jubilation followed. In the immediate aftermath of the game, Little gave a radio interview as part of a national broadcast. His first words were, "Hello to all my friends in Leominster."[85] It is said, by those who still remember, that Little's greeting created a collective cheer in the center of his hometown that could be heard through windows closed against January's cold. Football columnists and fans weighed in far and wide. Sportswriter Bill Henry summed up Columbia's performance as "Machine like, letter perfect, magnificently drilled, beautifully conditioned. Columbia was all of those things and more." New York-based United Press reported on January 2:

> The same jubilation that spread among the Israelites when David plunked Goliath with a pebble prevailed in Eastern football circles today because of Columbia's amazing Rose Bowl victory over Stanford.[86]

Some of the critics who had decried big time college football just weeks before found a way to celebrate the triumph of intelligent football players over raw brawn. As the team journeyed back east, well-wishers met their train at stations across America. Crowds assembled to catch a glimpse of football history, in some cases even if the train wasn't scheduled to stop. A stop in Boone, Iowa, on January 6 captured some of the joy:

---

83 *Los Angeles Times*, January 2, 1934.
84 *San Mateo Times*, January 2, 1934.
85 *Leominster Enterprise*, January 2, 1934.
86 *Syracuse Herald*, January 2, 1934.

> Still in a triumphant mood after their Rose Bowl victory,
> the Columbia University football squad passed through
> here en route home today. While the train changed
> crews here, the team amused a score of spectators with
> a spirited snowball fight. There were no casualties.[87]

When the football warriors' train arrived in Manhattan on the evening of January 8, five thousand fans were waiting. The reception included a motorcade escort home. Both sides of Broadway were lined with honking cars and cheering fans as the motorcycle police led the way. When the team reached Morningside Heights, the Columbia gymnasium was filled to double its capacity. Mayor Fiorello LaGuardia, sworn into office while the team was in California, provided New York's official welcome.[88]

Little had one more welcome in store. On January 17, 1934, Lou Little arrived by train at Worcester's Union Station. As he stepped off the platform, he gazed at a large crowd. It took him a few minutes to realize that the assembly was there to see him. A cavalcade led the victorious coach from Worcester to Leominster for a banquet in his honor that evening. By the time of arrival, the whole town had emptied out into Monument Square.[89] Fire alarms, church bells, factory whistles, and the cheers of thousands created a symphonic welcome for a man well on his way to a legendary career.[90]

Columbia's victory came at a time when the nation was desperate to believe in underdogs. Football's appeal has always resided in part in the potential triumph of the underestimated, the underrated, and the undersized. The 1934 Rose Bowl will always represent the value of earnest effort, hard work, and conviction. Every successful journey,

---

87 *Syracuse Herald*, January 7, 1934.
88 *Syracuse Herald*, January 8, 1934
89 *Leominster Enterprise,* January 17, 1934
90 In 1935, Lou Little joined John Heisman and Jim Crowley, one of the Notre Dame's Four Horsemen, on a panel appointed by New York's Downtown Athletic Club to approve a trophy design for the award given to college football's most outstanding player. The trophy was renamed in Heisman's honor the following year when the famous coach (and organizer of the Downtown Athletic Club) died. Wittingham, *Rites of Autumn: The Story of College Football*, 236.

whatever the challenge, starts with a belief in a goal. The Columbia Lions of 1933 symbolized courage for all of America at a time when that attribute was most needed. The economic depression posed challenges to all Americans. The country was undergoing great changes and the shifts caused a good deal of tumult. There was much to sort out. The country would have to adapt.

── *Chapter 7:* ──

Gangsters and Folk Heroes

During the 1930s Depression, many Americans, nearly helpless against forces they didn't understand, made heroes of outlaws who took what they wanted at gunpoint. Of all the lurid desperadoes, one man, John Hebert Dillinger, came to evoke this Gangster era, and stirred mass emotion to a degree rarely seen in this country.

—*From the official Federal Bureau of Investigation Web site,*
December 2009

In 1933, now-legendary gangsters roamed America, committing robberies and murders on an unprecedented scale. The most infamous included George "Baby Face" Nelson, John Dillinger, Charles Arthur "Pretty Boy" Floyd, Bonnie Parker, Clyde Barrow, and George "Machine Gun" Kelly. All of them, except Kelly, remained at large when the year ended. The exploits of these brazen criminals filled the same newspapers that carried accounts of the Leominster and Fitchburg football teams. The young men who took to the gridiron were experiencing a world turned upside down. The gangsters who challenged law enforcement in 1933 were no small part of the disruption of society.

The nation's lawmen faced huge challenges in the early 1930s. Some among their ranks would establish reputations equal in magnitude to their quarry. The Department of Investigation (DOI), as the future FBI was called in 1933, was headed by J. Edgar Hoover. He joined the agency at twenty-six years old in August 1922 as assistant director. He was elevated to director on May 10, 1924.

Agents of the DOI got a popular moniker during the tumultuous days of 1933. On September 26, 1933, three days after Fitchburg and Leominster high schools had achieved victory in their first football contests of the year, federal agents and local police cornered fugitives George and Kathryn Kelly at a residence in Memphis, Tennessee. Legend has it that Machine Gun Kelly, being unarmed, shouted, "Don't shoot, G-Men, don't shoot." Whether Kelly coined the shorthand for "government men" or not, the term stuck. Less than three weeks after their arrests, the Kellys were convicted and sentenced to life imprisonment for their part in the conspiracy to kill wealthy Oklahoma businessman Charles F. Urschel. George Kelly died of a heart attack at Leavenworth Penitentiary on July 17, 1954, the only one of the aforementioned gangsters to die of natural causes. Kathryn Kelly was released from a Cincinnati prison in 1958.

The G-Men did not formally become the FBI until July 1, 1935. The federal lawmen of 1933 lacked significant public support, while their notable targets enjoyed a certain mystique. The public, whose faith in public institutions was severely shaken by America's economic collapse, did not view bank robbery and bootlegging with the same level of disdain that might accompany those activities during more normal times. Despair was everywhere. Nearly one-third of the American workforce was unemployed. The nation's banks were failing; those that remained open were foreclosing on their borrowers in record numbers. Farm prices were dropping year by year and farms failed at historic and numbing rates. In the first five years of the 1930s, approximately 750,000 farms were lost to bank foreclosures or tax sales.[91] Neither the banks nor the ongoing prohibition of alcohol were in great favor with ordinary Americans. One stanza from a song of the era more than hinted at a division between classes in the nation:

---

91 Meltzer, *Brother Can You Spare A Dime?*, 91.

> I don't want your Rolls-Royce mister
> I don't want your pleasure yacht
> All I want is food for my babies
> Give me my old job back[92]

The marauding felons of 1933 quickly gained mythical status even as their crime sprees continued. The FBI's official Web site recounts the history of the gangster era:

> In the late 1920s through the 1930s, numerous high-profile crimes and criminals took center stage with J. Edgar Hoover and his agents, who became known as "G-Men." Gangsters, in particular, became larger than life, capturing the imagination of millions of Americans. Gangsters like "Machine Gun" Kelly, "Pretty Boy" Floyd, "Baby Face" Nelson, John Dillinger, Al Capone, "Ma" Barker, and others became notorious heroes.

Law enforcement had to play catch-up. Agents needed both an image boost and some practical law-enforcement tools to succeed in restoring order during the raucous years of the Great Depression. Meaningful help would not come until 1934. With the exception of Kelly, the majority of the notorious gangsters were at large at the end of 1933.

On May 18, 1934, Congress enacted a series of six crime-control measures. One of the new laws provided for the death penalty in cases of interstate kidnapping. Another law created a new federal crime: interfering with or assaulting federal law enforcement officers. A month later, federal special agents were given both the power of arrest as well as the right to carry firearms. Previously, federal agents had to rely on local police or U.S. Marshals to effect arrests.[93] J. Edgar Hoover and his G-Men now had a fighting chance.

Hoover's plan included shaping a new image for his agents. With the assistance of Hollywood and detective novelists, G-Men became brave crime fighters and the gangsters were recast as public enemies. The killing of Kansas City's police chief Otto Reed, two of his officers, and federal agent R.J. Caffrey on June 17, 1933, was a catalyst for change.

---

92 Meltzer, *Brother Can You Spare A Dime?*, 21.
93 http://www.fbi.gov/libref/historic/history/historicdates.htm, 3

The attack, carried out by Pretty Boy Floyd and his gang was intended to free an accomplice, Frank Nash, from prison.[94] The killings became known as the "Kansas City Massacre." Public opinion would no longer countenance unchecked and brazen violent crime.

The new powers and enhanced image of the FBI paid dividends in 1934. Gangsters Dillinger, Nelson, Floyd, Parker, and Barrow, all of whom had operated with impunity in 1933, would not survive 1934. Parker and Barrow were the first to die. The couple was believed to be responsible for thirteen murders and a string of robberies, burglaries, and kidnappings. Parker was nineteen when she met the twenty-one-year-old Barrow in 1930. She was married, he was not. Parker's husband was imprisoned for murder. Shortly after they met, Barrow was incarcerated for burglary. He was able to escape with a gun smuggled to him by Parker. After his recapture, Barrow was paroled in February 1932. He soon rejoined his later legendary partner in a shared life of crime.

Federal agents were after the infamous couple as a result of the comparatively petty charge of interstate auto theft in December 1932. An intense joint investigation by federal and local law enforcement in the spring of 1934 located the pair in a remote section of Louisiana. In the predawn hours of May 23, 1934, police officers from Louisiana and Texas staked out a rural highway in Sailes, Louisiana. Shortly after 8:00 AM, Clyde, wearing a blue silk suit, and Bonnie, in a red dress, purchased sandwiches at a breakfast café and drove toward the stakeout point where officers were hiding in the brush. When Clyde suspected that a breakdown on the road was a ruse, he moved his car forward to evade the police. The officers opened fire, pumping a barrage of 150 rounds into the Ford and its occupants. The legendary criminal couple were no more.[95]

Just six weeks later, another American crime legend met a similarly dramatic end. John Dillinger, more than any other gangster that prowled the American landscape in 1933, was a genuine celebrity who captured the public imagination. Dillinger was deemed "Public

---

94 Burrough, *Public Enemies: America's Great Crime Wave and the Birth of the FBI, 1933-1934*, 519. Nash was seated in Caffrey's Chevrolet with Chief Reed and agents Lackey and Smith. Nash was killed by gunfire from the gangsters. Smith was not hurt, but Lackey was seriously wounded.

95 Burrough, *Public Enemies: America's Great Crime Wave and the Birth of the FBI, 1933-1934*, 359.

Enemy Number One" on his thirty-first birthday, June 22, 1934, the announcement made by J. Edgar Hoover himself. The FBI director's action was calculated. Hoover was well aware of the reputation the notorious gangster had earned—a reputation that wasn't primarily negative. Dillinger had become an instant part of American folklore. Americans, feeling powerless, were attracted to the charismatic bank robber who dared take from institutions that were not in great favor with ordinary citizens.

The youth of the 1930s, perhaps more than previous generations, needed heroes. If gangsters like John Dillinger ever held their imagination, their popularity would be fleeting. The football players who lined up for Leominster and Fitchburg in 1933 primarily looked up to prominent sports figures of their day. Their boyhoods were filled with newspaper headlines and radio broadcasts detailing exploits of a Golden Age of sports. One of the nation's greatest sports legends was New York Yankees' slugger, Babe Ruth.

The "Sultan of Swat" dominated his sport like no other athlete. Before the 1933 season began, Ruth had completed nineteen years in major league baseball. To that point, he had hit 652 home runs and played in ten World Series. His most recent World Series appearance in 1932 was a Yankees' sweep of the Chicago Cubs. Ruth and teammate Lou Gehrig powered the Yanks over the outmatched Cubbies. The third game of the series, played at Chicago's Wrigley Field, featured one of the Babe's most legendary at-bats.

In the fifth inning, Ruth stepped up to the plate, facing the Cubs' Charlie Rout. The slugger heard the jeers of Cubs' fans from the right field stands and now faced more derision as he stood at the plate. Two lemons had been hurled his way during his first at-bat and a third piece of fruit was thrown in his direction during the fifth-inning plate appearance. With a count of two balls and two strikes, Ruth pointed, and according to Gehrig who waited on the deck circle, said, "I'm going to knock the next one down your goddamn throat." Where the slugger pointed has been debated ever since. Ruth launched the next pitch into the air, crushing a long home run to the right of the centerfield scoreboard. Thus the legend of the "called shot" home run was born.[96]

---

96 Montville, *The Big Bam: The Life and Time of Babe Ruth*, 310-311.

The 1933 season was different. Ruth was thirty-nine years old and his durability was in question. The economic climate, coupled with team worries about his longevity, dictated a salary reduction. Ruth signed a new contract on March 23, seventeen days after the president declared a bank holiday. The slugger's salary was cut from $75,000 to $52,000. Gehrig suffered a $5,000 pay decrease, signing a new contract paying him $22,500. Ruth managed to hit thirty-four home runs in 1933 and notch a .301 batting average. But the Yankees failed to win the pennant, finishing the season seven games behind the Washington Senators.

Ruth's home run total in 1933 was second in the American League to the As' Jimmy Foxx, who hit forty-eight. Lou Gehrig placed third in the league with thirty-two homers. Foxx also led the league in batting with a .356 average. Ruth accomplished two other significant feats in 1933: he hit the first home run in the inaugural All-Star Game at Chicago's Comiskey Park, helping the American League to a 4–2 victory, and he surprised fans when he pitched a complete game in a 6–5 victory over the Red Sox in the final game of the season—the last time he ever took the mound in the majors.

The 1933 World Series, which started on Tuesday, October 3 at New York's Polo Grounds, featured another New York City ball club, the Giants. As the Giants and the Senators faced off, the nation's most wanted man was wanted no more—he sat in the Allen County Jail in Lima, Ohio. Dillinger bet on the Giants.[97] As baseball's fall classic unfolded, the football squads of Leominster and Fitchburg readied for the third week of the season. The Giants, a heavy underdog, considered by many to be a second-rate ball club, scrapped their way to the National League pennant. 1933 was a year for underdogs apparently, as the Giants went on to beat the Senators in five games. Dillinger won his bet. While the Giants' heroes, among them tall southpaw Carl Hubbell and homer-hitting Mel Ott, basked in the glow of a new championship, Dillinger plotted a return to glory.

Dillinger had been held at the Lima jail since his arrest in Dayton, Ohio on September 22, 1933. When the gangster was frisked during his apprehension, police found a scrap of paper that appeared to show

97 http://www.johndillinger.com/aboutjohn-dillinger-menu-33/original-public-enemy.

a prison break plan. On September 26, eight members of the Dillinger gang escaped from the Indiana State Prison using the same plan found on Dillinger. A shotgun and several rifles had been smuggled into their cells. Three of the escapees showed up at the Lima jail on October 12. Impersonating Indiana State Prison authorities, they informed the Lima sheriff that they were there to take Dillinger to Indiana for a parole violation. The sheriff asked for credentials. In response came a bullet and a beating. The gang took the sheriff's keys, freed Dillinger, and left the sheriff to die, after locking his wife and deputy in a cell.[98]

The Dillinger gang ran wild during the fall of 1933. The Chesterfield-smoking, Schlitz-drinking Dillinger and his band committed several bank robberies, stole machine guns from police arsenals at the Indiana towns of Auburn and Peru, and killed two police officers during robberies in Chicago and East Chicago, Indiana. On January 23, 1934, Dillinger and three of his confederates were hiding out at a hotel in Tucson, Arizona. Their cover was blown when a fireman responding to a furnace fire at the hotel recognized the infamous guest from a detective magazine. The local police were summoned and Dillinger and his three fellow gangsters were taken into custody. The police seized three Thompson submachine guns, two Winchester rifles modified as machine guns, five bulletproof vests, and twenty-five thousand dollars in cash.[99]

Dillinger was lodged in the Crown Point, Indiana jail to await trial on a charge of murdering the East Chicago, Indiana police officer. The jailers boasted that their prison was escape-proof. Their prisoner had other ideas. With resource and cunning, Dillinger carved a wooden gun from the frame of a washboard. A coat of black shoe polish added the finishing touch. On March 3, 1934, Dillinger forced guards to open his cell using the fake gun. Once outside his cell, he grabbed two machine guns, locked up the guards and a number of prison officials, and sped off in a stolen sheriff's car.

Once the fleeing felon drove the stolen car across the state line from Indiana to Illinois, the federal authorities had their jurisdiction. The manhunt for Dillinger took agents to St. Paul, Minnesota, upper

---

98 Burrough, *Public Enemies: America's Greatest Crime Wave and the Birth of the FBI, 1933-1934*, 142.

99 Burrough, *Public Enemies: America's Greatest Crime Wave and the Birth of the FBI, 1933-1934*, 199–200.

Michigan, and Wisconsin. During the four months after his Crown Point escape, Dillinger robbed banks, got in shoot-outs with police, and narrowly escaped special agents twice. Dillinger was wounded in his first encounter with the G-Men on March 31 at St. Paul. The wounded gangster recuperated in the company of his girlfriend Evelyn Frechette, who joined him at Dillinger's father's home in Mooresville, Indiana.[100]

A break in the case came on July 21, 1934. Ana Cumpanas, alias Anna Sage, the madam of a Gary, Indiana brothel, had information to sell. Cumpanas wanted a cash reward and help with her deportation proceedings. The Department of Labor was in the process of sending Cumpanas back to Romania, from where she had emigrated in 1914. The madam met with the special agents in charge the Dillinger case, Samuel A. Cowley and Melvin Purvis. The agents agreed to pay her a reward for the gangster's capture and to inform the Department of Labor about her cooperation.

Cumpanas told Cowley and Purvis that Dillinger had visited her brothel with a girlfriend of hers, Polly Hamilton. She also informed the agents that the trio planned to go to the movies the following evening. Unsure of what Chicago theater they would attend, either the Biograph or Marbo, Cumpanas told the agents she would wear an orange dress to help them identify their quarry. The feds staked out both movie houses. On the evening of Sunday, July 22, Cumpanas, Hamilton, and Dillinger walked into the ice-cooled Biograph to watch *Manhattan Melodrama* starring Clark Gable. In accordance with Hoover's instructions, the G-Men waited until Dillinger emerged from the theater before closing in. Two hours after entering the Biograph, Dillinger exited with his two companions. Special Agent Purvis, standing in a nearby doorway, lit a cigarette to signal the other agents.

An alert Dillinger recognized the tip-off and ran for a nearby alley. Federal agents Charles B. Winstead, Clarence Hunt, and Herman E. Hollis fired a total of five shots at Public Enemy Number One. Three bullets hit Dillinger, and he collapsed face down. Less than twenty minutes later, the gangster who defined an era was pronounced dead at the Alexian Brothers Hospital.

---

100 Frechette was later arrested while in Chicago visiting a friend. She was tried and convicted in St. Paul for harboring a fugitive. Frechette was fined one thousand dollars and sentenced to two years in prison.

The lawlessness prevailing in America during 1933 was greatly curtailed the following year. 1933 was not only the depth of the Great Depression but also the pinnacle of many gangsters' careers. The youth of the land witnessed a time of despair, and heard mixed messages from a variety of influential public figures. It is difficult to imagine exactly what the impressionable high school football players of that year thought about the direction of the country they would soon inherit. Many were worried.

The working world they would soon enter was not stable. Joe Goodhue, who played left guard for Leominster High School's undefeated 1932 football team, graduated in the spring of 1933. The family business was impacted by the market crash and the failure of Leominster's National Bank. The Goodhue Company, operated by Joe's father, had manufactured diverse goods from horn since Joe's grandfather established the business in 1877. During the 1930s, the company's mainstay was fabricating handles for machetes used to harvest sugar cane in Puerto Rico, Cuba, and parts of South America. The firm did not survive the 1930s, closing its doors in 1938. Competition from plastics and a considerable financial loss caused by a bank failure combined to spell the end. It is easier to appreciate the folk-hero status of bank robbers like Dillinger if a bank failure has cost you your life savings. Even today, the younger Goodhue, now ninety-five, has a certain glint in his eye when he ponders the curious charm of John Dillinger.

Like many Americans, the Goodhue family was not deterred by difficulty. Mom and Dad ran Goodhue's, a successful downtown Leominster restaurant and bakery from 1930 through 1958, where they pioneered wholesale distribution of frozen bread dough. The younger Goodhue, who studied business at the University of Pennsylvania's prestigious Wharton School and graduated in 1939, launched a long, diverse, and rewarding business career. In 1933 nothing was certain, but hope was not lost. Giving up was not an option. Survival required perseverance, resourcefulness, and hard work.

Nearly eight decades later, Joe Goodhue can remember the entrepreneurial spirit that helped supplement his family's income. As a young man, he distributed the *Saturday Evening Post* and the *Ladies' Home Journal*. During breaks from college, Goodhue organized and operated a day camp on Spectacle Pond where he instructed in swimming and outdoor games. Campers paid fifty cents per day, station wagon transportation included.

The Goodhues were fortunate: they survived and prospered. Elsewhere, others were not as fortunate. The idle went hungry. The unemployed longed for a purpose. Despair was palpable throughout America. Some of the forlorn just saw no way out. Louis Adamic, a writer, recounted a scene from Lawrence, Massachusetts:

> For several minutes I watched an elderly man who stood on a deserted corner near the enormous and idle Everett Mills in the posture of an undotted question mark. He did not see me. Every now and then he swung his arms, not because it was cold, but no doubt because he wanted activity other than walking around, which he probably had been doing for years in a vain effort to get a job. He mumbled to himself. Then, suddenly, he stepped off the curb and picked up a long piece of string from a pile of rubbish, and his big, work-eager hands began to work with it, tying and untying feverishly. He worked with the string for several minutes. Then he looked around and, seeing me, dropped the string, his haggard, hollow face coloring a little, as though from a sense of guilt, or intense embarrassment. He was shaken and confused and stood there for several seconds, looking down at the rubbish heap, then up at me. His hands finally dropped to his sides. Then his arms swung in a sort of idle reflex motion and he turned, hesitated a while as if he did not know where to go and finally shuffled off, flapping his arms. I noticed that his overcoat was split in the back and that his heels were worn off completely.[101]

Americans needed a distraction from the harsh reality of the times. Sports were as important as movies, newsreels, or the parlor radio, and often provided the grist for all of those mediums. Football, a gritty, unflinching American game, was a tonic for a weary population.

---

101 Meltzer, *Brother Can You Spare a Dime?* 16.

— Chapter 8: —

Fitchburg's Football Season

Fitchburg High School's team continued its season with the same determination that it brought to its initial game with Keene. By 1933, Fitchburg had developed a fine tradition of football success. It was coach Amiott's twenty-first season at the helm of the Red and Gray. He earned his appointment as head football coach and athletic director just a year after graduating from FHS. When Amiott retired in 1937, he had a lifetime winning percentage of .724. His record against archrival Leominster was even more impressive. The Red and Gray under Amiott posted a record of 17-4-2 against Leominster through 1932. (In some of those seasons, the rivals met more than once.)

Uncertain times placed a greater reliance on traditions, which meant football was even more important in 1933. The young men who had a chance to compete on the gridiron knew they were privileged to have the opportunity. The community that supported them took pride in their team and welcomed the diversion that football brought that autumn. The atmosphere was charged with excitement. The city was hopeful.

Fitchburg hosted the Lynn General Electric Apprentices for the second game of the 1933 season. In the newspaper style of the day, the *Sentinel* summed the game up in two acerbic paragraphs:

94

> Using high tension power, Fitchburg High defeated
> Lynn General Electric Apprentices 21 to 0 at Crocker
> Field Saturday afternoon. Fitchburg gave a brilliant
> display of polished, flashy line plays and end runs.
>
> Instead of depending on an aerial attack, which
> Lynn evidently anticipated, Fitchburg "crossed wires"
> and shocked the visitors with power and speed to score
> in each of the first three periods. Lynn was not only
> held scoreless but failed to make a first down until the
> final period.

The article was accompanied by a box headlined "Short Circuited" that listed the players who saw action and gave a scoring summary. Bill Mackie scored two of Fitchburg's three touchdowns and all three of its extra points, accounting for fifteen of Fitchburg's twenty-one points. Mackie's impact on his new squad had been impossible to miss. Another tongue-in-cheek *Sentinel* column was headed "Electric Flashes." There the sports editor made a number of game notes. The cheering squad of Helen Niskala, Agnes Gorham, Jennie Savela, Roland Gendron, and John Duane gave an inspiring performance and "attracted much attention." The band under the direction of George Talcott played well and "… gave indications of soon being ready for marching movements." The editor also recorded what was already becoming obvious: "Bill Mackie is the fastest and biggest backfield player Fitchburg High has had in years and the plays assigned to that position click when he handles them." But a great deal of football remained. The Red and Gray readied to host their third opponent of the season, Providence Central High School, on Saturday, October 7.[102]

The Providence Central team represented a high school attended by thousands, formed by the merger of three high schools. Its administrators included two principals, an assistant principal, two deans of girls, and two chief advisers. Providence's coach Joe Curtin scouted the Red and Gray in their game with Lynn General Electric. He came away confident.

Saturday afternoon's crowd was a bit sparser than expected. Some fans stayed home, camped by their radios, listening to the New York

---

102 *Fitchburg Sentinel,* October 2, 1933.

Giants beat the Washington Senators in the fifth and deciding game of the World Series by a score of 11 to 4 in ten innings. The Fitchburg fans who filed into Crocker Stadium got an early scare. Providence returned the opening kickoff to their own twenty-seven-yard line. On the next play, Osmanski took the direct snap and crashed into the left side of the line. The fullback sliced though the line. Still on his feet, he broke the tackles of the remaining Fitchburg defenders and dashed seventy-three yards for the first score notched against the Red and Gray that year.

The Fitchburg faithful would soon be calmed. Their squad quickly overcame the 6–0 deficit with a good display of gridiron teamwork. The ball was distributed among all the backs. This time Mackie contributed more with his arm than with his legs. The southpaw pitcher also passed with his left arm. He can still recall the difficulty his left-handed passes caused defenders. Mackie's passes against Providence were on target. Long completions chewed up huge chunks of yardage for the Red and Gray. Most of the few passes which fell incomplete were dropped. The remaining Fitchburg backs were effective on the ground. Sophomore fullback Lauri Shattuck played brilliantly, crossing the goal line for Fitchburg four times. Halfbacks Mologhan and Mackie each scored one touchdown. Fitchburg routed Providence Central by the score of 39–8. Providence coach Joe Curtin quipped, "Gee, that Fitchburg has improved in a week." The *Sentinel* maintained its editorial style: the game notes were titled "Central Points" and the scoring box "Lowering the Curtin."

Coach Amiott savored victory only briefly. He had other things on his mind. "We hope for more improvement [next] week," stated the legendary coach. He knew that beating the next opponent, powerful Arlington High School, would require his team's optimum performance. Arlington was eager to face Fitchburg. The suburban Middlesex County school had already purchased eight hundred tickets a week before the game to be played at Fitchburg's Crocker Field. Arlington had handled the Red and Gray the season before, breaking a Fitchburg winning streak by routing the home team 32–0.

The veteran Arlington squad, led by coach Ostergren, arrived at Crocker Field on Saturday, October 14. Nine of Arlington's 1932 starters were back to meet the Red and Gray again. Fitchburg had only three returning starters in the lineup: co-captains (and brothers) Stanley and Felix Esielionis and left halfback Doug Mologhan. The game that followed was close, one of the tightest contests Fitchburg played all season.

Fitchburg struck first. The Red and Gray's first drive featured a long Mackie pass that netted more than thirty yards and a first down on the Arlington one-yard line. On the next play Mackie went around the left end to score the game's first touchdown. The versatile back added the extra point. Fitchburg led 7–0. Arlington capitalized on a Fitchburg mistake in the second period when the home team's quarterback fumbled a punt reception on his own twenty-yard line. Arlington recovered, and four plays later the visitors tied the game 7–7.

The first half ended without further scoring. The tandem of Mackie and Shattuck got the ball moving with solid ground gains in the third period. The two running backs alternated carries on a seven-play, sixty-yard drive which culminated with a Fitchburg touchdown. Once again, Mackie added the extra point and the Red and Gray lead once more, this time by the score of 14–7. The fourth quarter seesawed back and forth, neither team able to sustain its drives.

Finally, a Mackie punt went out of bounds on the Fitchburg forty-three-yard line. Arlington started its possession with a "Statue of Liberty" play that went for five yards. Arlington's quarterback Madden then completed a pass to left halfback McLean who advanced the ball to the Fitchburg fifteen. Lauri Shattuck made a saving tackle but injured his leg in the process. Arlington tested the Fitchburg line with Lane, their fullback, who gained only a yard. With just a minute left in the game, some of the crowd of seven thousand surged toward the River Street end zone where the impending drama was about to be played out. The officials held up play until the crowd could be moved back. When play resumed, the Arlington quarterback took the snap and looked toward McLean scampering toward the Fitchburg goal line. Madden passed into McLean's waiting hands. The receiver was tackled on the four-yard line having converted a first down. The next play resulted in offsetting offsides penalties. The clock permitted Arlington one more play. Madden surged quickly toward the Fitchburg line. Defensive tackle Felix Esielionis stopped the quarterback cold. The game ended with Arlington stalled on the Fitchburg ten-yard line. The Red and Gray had held off the late attack and preserved an important victory.

The Red and Gray approached the mid-point of their pre-Thanksgiving schedule on the crest of a successful streak. Fitchburg hosted Framingham for its fifth game. The visitors took both their pre-game lunch and post-game dinner at the Hotel Raymond. The two teams had started playing each other during the 1930 season. In previous meetings, Framingham had been able to hold the Red and Gray in check. That was not the case on Saturday, October 21, 1933. Bill Mackie's running talents were on full display. He scored two of Fitchburg's four touchdowns. Brodeur, Shattuck's back-up, scored the other two. Mackie booted three extra points and Framingham was shut out 27–0. Fitchburg was undefeated through its first five games.

As early as the aftermath of the Arlington game, sportswriters began the dialogue over a state title. The *Boston Herald* noted:

> The Fitchburg defeat of Arlington places Fitchburg among the title contenders. Fitchburg deserves plenty of credit. Any group capable of leading a good Arlington team deserves plenty of notice.[103]

The *Boston Globe* also speculated on the battle to claim a Massachusetts' title. "Saturday's results leave Fitchburg, Everett and Leominster in the van of state title contenders."[104] The Red and Gray had played half of the games leading up to the Thanksgiving duel with Leominster. Coach Amiott and the entire city were happy with the team's progress. Nevertheless, a lot of football remained. Despite the attention of the state's largest newspapers, nothing could be taken for granted during the remaining portion of the season.

The following Saturday, a line of cars paraded twelve miles from the West. "Lieut. Wallace and other motor vehicle officers escorted the Gardner automobiles throughout the city to be sure no excited youngster lost his head."[105] The Gardner faithful had made a custom of automobile parades to away games and the participants were safely guided to their parking area adjacent to Crocker field. Gardner's Mayor Timpany, city solicitor Livingston, and members of the city council were part of the traveling contingent. The visiting eleven from the Chair City,

103 *Boston Herald*, October 16, 1933.
104 *Boston Globe,* October 18, 1933.
105 *Fitchburg Sentinel,* October 30, 1933.

a name Gardner earned from its furniture manufacturing reputation, were led by coach Phillip J. Tarpey. Gardner was a small city in 1933, not one-third the size of Fitchburg. The Red and Gray respected their foe. The teams met on Saturday, October 28, and Fitchburg's regard for the visitors proved wisely held.

The Gardner defense was stout. The Wildcats' efforts limited the powerful Red and Gray offense to their smallest point total of the entire season. Bill Mackie, Fitchburg's greatest offensive weapon, was held in check for most of the game. The defensive effort was impressive, especially when the relative size of the schools was considered. Yet no one was really surprised. The Wildcat football tradition was a good one and their teams had played Fitchburg tough for many years.

When it was over, Fitchburg had prevailed, keeping its undefeated record intact. Mackie did figure in both of Fitchburg's touchdowns. The headline summarized the results:

Gardner Holds Fitchburg To Only Two Touchdowns
Wildcats Strong Defensively;
Forward Produces First Tally;
Mackie Bolts Through For Other

Fitchburg's first score was the result of a fifty-five-yard toss from Mackie to Johnson. The talented passer missed the extra point. The middle quarters of the game saw both teams struggle; neither was able to sustain a drive. The final quarter featured Fitchburg's second touchdown on a thirty-yard Mackie run off tackle. Mackie added the extra point, concluding scoring at 13-0. Across town in Leominster, the Blue and White defeated Framingham, a common foe with Fitchburg. The *Boston Herald* was already presaging a battle between the rivals. "What a fight these two will have on Thanksgiving."[106]

Fitchburg looked forward to November football. The Red and Gray faced four opponents before its scheduled Thanksgiving classic with Leominster. First up was Brookline High School on November 4. The Fitchburg players performed their pre-game warm-ups in their usual uniforms, but reappeared in their "striking" new red satin pants just in time for the game. The new attire brought a roar from the proud fans.

---

106 *Boston Herald,* October 31, 1933.

The novel uniforms caused fans to immediately debate over a fitting nickname. The most popular ideas were Redskins, Red Wings, Red Devils, and Red Dragons.

The conversation in the stands may have also involved politics. A hotly contested Fitchburg mayoral election loomed on Tuesday, November 7. Three-term incumbent Joseph N. Carriere met challenges from three other candidates. Frank W. Lesure, proprietor of the Palace Steam Laundry who like the mayor was a non-partisan, joined Robert E. Greenwood, nominee of the Independent-Progressive Party and Thomas Casey of the Citizens Party in the contest. Political sentiment ran high throughout Massachusetts. Governor Joseph Ely had appointed an election supervisor for Chelsea and ordered fifteen state police officers to protect voters. In Chelsea, state representative William H. Melley sought to unseat eight-term incumbent mayor Lawrence F. Quigley. The election was accompanied by beatings, a near riot, and the arrests of two men for impersonating voters. Melley claimed Chelsea was "infested by gunmen and racketeers."[107]

The Fitchburg mayoral election did not erupt in violence, but the campaign was vigorous and virulent. Greenwood provided the most significant challenge to Mayor Carriere. The Independent-Progressive campaigned on a charge of municipal mismanagement against the incumbent. He stated:

> I've made definitive recommendations, I've told you why I think the other candidates are inadequate. I've done it in time for rebuttal; no one has risen to refute my statements.[108]

Greenwood's message worked. He defeated Carriere in a close election, besting the incumbent by 136 votes. The narrow result triggered a recount; however, the Greenwood victory was upheld.[109] Campaign finances were also close. Carriere raised $600 in the losing effort, having received $450 from city solicitor A. A. Gelinas, $50 from

---

107 *Fitchburg Sentinel*, November 14, 1933.

108 *Fitchburg Sentinel*, November 6, 1937.

109 Greenwood's total tally was 5,103 votes. The incumbent Carriere garnered 4,967 votes. Lesure came in third with 3,281 and Casey trailed with 126. The recount only netted two additional votes for Carriere.

Dr. J. A. N. Thibeault, and $100 from Xavier Morin. The winner raised $220 from attorney Samuel Salney and $425 from former mayor M. Fred O'Connell.[110]

The Saturday contest before the election on the football field (featuring the dazzling new pants) was not as close. The Red and Gray dominated the visitors from Brookline. The *Sentinel* byline reported "Visitors Appear Woefully Weak Against Red and Gray, Which Registered Six Touchdowns." Brookline was held scoreless. The local newspaper continued: "*Redskins* line again shows great power while backs perform sensationally."[111] Fitchburg scored twice in each of the first three quarters on their way to a 38–0 victory. Fitchburg's reserves threatened several times in the final period but Brookline held. The visitors never penetrated closer than the Fitchburg forty-six.

Despite the complete domination, the Red and Gray could not exult in the victory or their undefeated 7–0 record. Fitchburg's next contest was their first away game. The opponent was the mighty Brockton High School, the "Shoe Makers." A bit of Fitchburg's thunder was stolen by Malden's defeat of Brockton on November 4. A strong Malden team had beaten Brockton on Malden's home field. Going into Brockton's Keith Field and stealing away victory was another matter.

The recently rechristened "Redskins" moved the ball against Brockton in the first stanza but could not finish the drive for points. The second quarter started with Fitchburg in good field position at the Shoe Makers' twenty-four-yard line. Fitchburg ran off two plays and managed six yards. On the next play, Brockton defender Chesnauskos broke through the Fitchburg interference and the Red and Gray lost four yards. While sprawled on the ground, Bill Mackie's hand was penetrated by a cleat. Mackie was in pain and time was called. Once again, Fitchburg's left halfback played through an injury. Perhaps because of his lip injury in the first game, Mackie was the lone Fitchburg player to wear a facemask that season. Coach Amiott required it. This second injury would require a shot of horse serum to prevent lockjaw, given once the game had concluded.

---

110 It is probably no surprise that Salney replaced Gelinas as Mayor Greenwood's city solicitor.

111 *Fitchburg Sentinel,* November 6, 1933.

Mackie returned to the game without missing a play. The first play after the timeout was a lateral from the fullback Brodeur to Mackie who then lateralled again to the left end Johnson. Johnson battled across the Brockton goal line, scoring the game's first touchdown. The Red and Gray added a second touchdown in the third period on the strength of Mackie's arm. The southpaw passer completed an eighteen-yard strike to left end Leo and then a seventy-three-yard toss to right end Johnson for the score. The Red and Gray scored a third touchdown later. A Mackie pass was caught by Leo, who in turn lateralled to fullback Brodeur. Brodeur was forced "outside" (out of bounds) by the defenders of the home team. On the very next play, Brodeur cracked the Shoe Makers' line and went into their goal standing up. Mackie made his first try after of the day and the score stood at 19–0.

The final quarter featured the play of several Fitchburg reserves. Early in the period, co-captain Stanley Esielionis recovered a fumble on the Brockton nineteen. The Fitchburg offense moved the ball to the Brockton eight-yard line after a nine-yard pass to Leo and a Brodeur two-yard plunge. On the next play, Fitchburg lost the ball on a touchback by passing the ball incomplete into the Brockton end zone. Under the rules of the day, a forward pass falling incomplete in the defenders' end zone resulted in a touchback for the defenders. The ball went over to Brockton at their twenty-yard line.

Before the day was done, Fitchburg scored a fourth touchdown and Brockton crossed the goal line once. The final score was Fitchburg 26, Brockton 6. It was the first time Brockton had lost at home in thirty-five games. The Malden defeat of Brockton the week before was the Shoe Makers' first loss anywhere in twenty-two contests. Fitchburg's victory was the worst defeat ever suffered by Brockton at Keith Field.[112]

The same edition of the *Sentinel* that carried the news of the victory over Brockton featured two front-page stories regarding liquor. By November 1933 the nation expected the repeal of Prohibition. States, including Massachusetts, debated the form of laws regulating the sale of liquor in their legislatures. The *Sentinel* reported that Mrs. Frank P. Bennet, representing sixty-five thousand women for the Massachusetts State Federation of Women's Clubs, objected to the licensing of taverns. Mrs. Bennet stated, "Repealists told us there would be no return of

---

112 *Fitchburg Sentinel*, November 13, 1933.

the saloon. Let's not break the faith. Taverns are modified saloons. Lawlessness and crime will come in their wake …"[113]

It is no secret that Prohibition did not stop the use of liquor. Sadly, the same front page featured a story on the tragic death of twenty-year-old John Robinson of Worcester. Robinson was a popular student and athlete at the Fitchburg Teacher's College. The sophomore was celebrating the end of the soccer season with six other players at a camp on Spec Pond in Leominster. One of the players went to obtain alcohol. The young man who was to supply the liquor was not home when the player called. After a brief conversation with the supplier's father, a can was found in the cellar which was assumed to be the alcohol intended for the party. Unfortunately, the can contained methanol for use in an automobile radiator. By the time the mistake was discovered by the frantic father, Robinson could not be saved.

Prohibition was formally repealed on December 5, 1933, with Utah's ratification of the Twenty-First Amendment. The rush to obtain liquor licenses was on, and the competition caused immediate problems for the new mayor, Robert Greenwood, and Fitchburg. In his inaugural address on January 2, 1934, Mayor Greenwood called the action of the existing license commission "outrageous." Wasting no time, he appointed what became known as the "New Board." Undaunted, the "Old Board" continued its work under Louis N. M. Deschenes, its chairman, despite being ousted from city hall. The Old Board took up an office on the second floor of the Johnsonia building. For a number of months, the city had two licensing boards acting independently of each other. The whole matter ended up before the Massachusetts Supreme Court, which ruled in favor of the "Old Board," dismissing Greenwood's theory that the preexisting board appointed by Mayor Carriere was not legally formed because its members were never confirmed by the city council.

In the midst of the chaos, one establishment, to be operated at 43 Lunenburg Street, actually applied for a restaurant liquor license to each of the boards. The Old Board allowed the petition of Earl J. Remick for a common victualer's license but denied his application for a liquor permit. Before the restaurant was opened, Remick's interest was transferred to Daniel F. Slattery. Slattery applied and was given a liquor

113 *Fitchburg Sentinel*, November 13, 1933.

permit by the "New Board," the very first one they issued prior to being disbanded by the court decision.[114]

The flurry of activity over the impending repeal of Prohibition did nothing to derail the hopes of Fitchburg High School's vaunted football team. Next up after Brockton was Quincy High School. Once again the Red and Gray were the hosts. Quincy, despite an early season demolishing by Leominster, was an improved team and the Red and Gray could not afford to let their guard down.

The field for the Quincy game was soft and ready to be churned into a morass of slippery mud. The squad B-game between Fitchburg and Gardner the Monday before had been canceled, as more than an inch and a half of snow blanketed Crocker Field. The following Thursday, the field froze when the mercury dropped to a local record low of four degrees. The week's weather was an ideal recipe for bad footing on Saturday.

Soon after kickoff, Crocker Field was a muddy quagmire. Mackie and his mud-spattered teammates led the barely discernable Red and Gray to a dominant lead. The Fitchburg team posted twenty-one points and shut out Quincy. Fitchburg earned nineteen first downs to one for the Granite City gridders.

Coach Amiott pulled Mackie and the entire first team in the third quarter. Amiott had an eye toward Thanksgiving Day and Leominster. The Fitchburg mentor wasn't taking any chances. Mackie had been wearing face protection the entire season. Shattuck, who had his leg in a cast as a result of a knee injury suffered against Arlington on October 14, was available to play at Brockton and again in the Quincy game. But Amiott saved the talented sophomore. Two other Fitchburg starters, Brodeur and Johnson, wore nose guards. Johnson had broken his nose in the Brockton game. With the Fitchburg starters out of the game, Quincy was able to score two touchdowns, both on interception returns.

---

114 *Fitchburg Sentinel,* February 12, 1934. Slattery had to apply for an "original license" on August 20, 1934 to the old and legal board (*Fitchburg Sentinel,* August 20, 1934). He was granted a restaurant liquor permit; however, trouble was not far behind. His restaurant permit was suspended for having inadequate kitchen facilities (*Fitchburg Sentinel,* September, 14, 1934). Slattery was allowed a tavern license after a two-day suspension (*Fitchburg Sentinel,* September 17, 1934).

But Amiott's gamble did not backfire. Fitchburg prevailed 21–13 to remain unbeaten. After Quincy, Fitchburg had one final home game before traveling to Leominster's Doyle Field for what was fast becoming the most anticipated game of the state's high school football season.

The last team to visit Crocker Field in 1933 was Chicopee High School. The Fitchburg-Chicopee meeting was a benefit game. Proceeds from ticket sales were used for relief of the city's poor. The want and despair that gripped the nation was also present in Fitchburg. Volunteer efforts to ease the burden of the unfortunate were common. Citizens banded together to aid neighbors who suffered the most. In the past, game tickets, which cost an adult twenty-five cents and school children a dime, were distributed door-to-door by high school students. The students were able to canvass the entire city in one hour. The 1933 effort was expanded to the entire student population of the city. Everyone got caught up in the spirit of the cause. The game officials, players, band, ushers, and ticket-takers all bought tickets to the game.

The large crowd that filed into Crocker Field for the Chicopee game on November 25 included Leominster head coach Charles Broderick, assistant coach Ted Kucharski, and the entire Leominster football team. The Blue and White had no game on the Saturday before Thanksgiving and they were invited guests of Fitchburg that day. For the second week in a row, the playing surface at historic Crocker Field was soft and muddy. Coach Amiott decided to save his team's new red uniforms, which included the silk pants, for the biggest game of the season with Leominster. Fitchburg's Redskins suited up in white uniforms. Some players wore different numbers, and fans had a bit of difficulty initially identifying the Fitchburg players.

The game was never close. Fitchburg defeated Chicopee in a complete rout. Five different Fitchburg players scored touchdowns. Despite the easy win, Bill Mackie did briefly draw the ire of Amiott. Seventy-six years later, it is the only time the dynamic football star of 1933 ever remembers upsetting his legendary coach. Amiott was a man of even temper, universally considered a consummate gentleman. He was not prone to displays of anger. The play that upset the coach involved Mackie catching up with his blocker Bernard Mologhan during a breakaway run, so he could hand the ball to Mologhan, allowing him to claim the score. Mackie didn't realize he was competing for the state's scoring record. His coach was hoping to ensure that his left halfback earned the top honor. Mackie scored thirty-four points that Saturday, five touchdowns and four points after. After the game, Mackie had the lead in the race for the state scoring title. Mackie posted 128 points, leading Salem's Timmy Mavrakos's 114 points through November 25. The undefeated Red and Gray, who beat Chicopee 60–0, led the state in team scoring. Fitchburg outscored its first ten opponents in 1933 by a mark of 278–34.

Only one hurdle remained. Fitchburg's season hinged on one final game. Despite the overwhelming success the team had experienced, the season could not conclude satisfactorily without a defeat of rival Leominster on Thanksgiving Day. A loss to the Blue and White would tarnish the significant accomplishments of one of Fitchburg's greatest teams. Fitchburg practiced on the Monday and Tuesday before Thanksgiving. The team worked hard perfecting its game plan for Leominster. The team moved its practices off Crocker Field, the surface of which had degraded further with more rain and warm weather. The *Sentinel* captured the attitude succinctly in the very first entry of the "Sports Chatter column": "Leominster Next!"[115]

---

115 *Fitchburg Sentinel*, November 27, 1933.

Chapter 9:

Leominster's Season

For its second game of the season, the Leominster High School football team hosted Athol at Doyle Field on September 30, 1933. Leominster was a heavy favorite. The Blue and White had not lost a game since Thanksgiving 1931. LHS was undefeated and untied in 1932, outscoring its opponents 205–12. The result of the first contest of 1933, in which Leominster dominated Quincy 46–0, was still reverberating throughout the state.

The boys from the "Tool City" played hard but they were no match for Leominster. Ronnie Cahill, Leominster's triple-threat left halfback, turned in a remarkable performance. Displaying all of his talents, Cahill ran for two of Leominster's five touchdowns and threw three touchdown passes to account for the remaining six-pointers. His punts helped hold Athol scoreless. Leominster converted two extra points, one on a Cahill run and the other, the only point Cahill did not figure in, was a lateral pass from quarterback Daniel Bell to Caisse who scampered into the end zone. The scoreboard's final tally was Leominster 32, Athol 0.

As the calendar turned to October, Leominster readied itself to face tough competition from schools willing to schedule them. Many of the high schools were some distance away and one of the opponents was a

Rhode Island team. Apart from the gridiron, the ebb and flow of life in the city continued despite the difficult times.

During the first week of October, political campaigning was in the air. Sidney Bell became the first candidate to take out nomination papers for mayor in the election scheduled for December 5. His first run for mayor in 1925 had been unsuccessful. Bell lost his first bid to Bernard W. Doyle, a Leominster industrialist, civic leader, and philanthropist. Doyle donated Leominster's football stadium to the city in 1929 and announced his retirement from politics in the fall of the same year. Bell returned to politics, winning and retaining a seat as a councilor at large by a wide margin in the 1929 and 1931 elections.[116]

While local politics geared up in early October, the Leominster district court digested a variety of cases characteristic of the times. Judge Ralph J. Robbins sentenced an eighteen-year-old Peterson Street man who was convicted of stealing a bushel of potatoes from a city garden operated by Leominster's Welfare Department at the Snow farm on Wachusett Street. The "hot potatoes" earned the man fifteen days in the house of correction. After disposing of a drunk driving charge by a fifty-dollar fine (the defendant was given three months to pay), the judge took up the case of Brockelman Brothers' Food Market. The complaint against the popular downtown food market charged that "Brockelman Bros., Inc., Sept. 21 did sell to one Henry C. Mossman for food, certain tainted, corrupt, decayed and unwholesome hamburg steak." The product sold for about fifteen cents per pound. Under the examination of defense counsel James R. Oliver (who ran for mayor unsuccessfully that year), store manager Fred Seuss testified that he had consumed the suspected product both raw and cooked with no ill effect, pronouncing the hamburg wholesome. The judge was not persuaded; he fined the store fifty dollars.[117]

On Saturdays in the autumn of 1933, civic concerns were put aside for football. Excitement for the local gridiron teams peaked as game

---

116 Bell won the race for Mayor on December 5, 1933, outpolling two challengers, attorney James Oliver and Lester H. Gove, the former president of the Leominster Taxpayers Association. Incumbent mayor Fredrick Platt did not run for reelection. Bell's vote totaled 3,849; Oliver polled 2,086 and Gove 543 votes.

117 *Fitchburg Sentinel*, October 9, 1933.

day arrived. The first game in October 1933 was against the always-competitive Amesbury High School. Leominster school officials had long respected the Amesbury program, so much so that they recruited the Amesbury coach in 1931 when Leominster's incumbent coach Raymond Comeford tragically drowned in August of that year.

Charles Broderick's arrival in Leominster was not smooth. He replaced a very popular coach under difficult circumstances, and at least a few members of the athletic council were not supportive of his hiring. When the coach lost three of his first four games, trouble brewed.[118]

On the morning of October 29, 1931, the coach struck back in the newspaper and on the practice field. Leominster got its first taste of "C.B.," as he was affectionately known in later years. In an unequivocal and stingingly direct statement, the coach spoke to the *Leominster Enterprise*:

> There is no room for any 90 per centers on this squad. If the boys are not out here to fight with their team 100 per cent they can just turn in their suits and consider their athletic career at Leominster High School at an end. I am here to put a football team on the field and if the boys in the high school are not loyal enough to give me their support we'll have a team just the same. I'll put on a team if I have to go down to the Junior High School for material and play before a crowd of nine men and a police officer. I am here to put out a team and if any civilians who are not satisfied and are not man enough to come to me personally and register their complaint let them hold their peace and not poison the minds of a group of School boys to lie down on their school, their city and their own decency and self-respect. I am here to coach this team in my own way. I was hired to put a group of football players on the field but I cannot do it unless I get 100 per cent cooperation. I would rather have a dozen dubs that were playing with

118 One of those losses came at the hands of his old team Amesbury High on October 24, 1931. His former players presented him with a gold chain and pocket knife at midfield before the game, as well as the 12–7 loss.

all they had than a group of temperamental athletes who are not out to fight all the time. I am going through with my contract to give this school the best coaching I can, regardless of any adverse pressure or sore-headed friction.[119]

The 1932 undefeated season and two important wins to commence 1933 had erased all questions concerning Broderick. The coach prepared for a contest against Amesbury. He knew the game would be hard-fought and well played.

Broderick's inklings were correct. The Amesbury game was Leominster's first real test of 1933. Leominster opened the scoring in the first period. After a touchdown run by Cahill was called back for a penalty, Leominster held the ball at the Amesbury thirty-one-yard line. The left end, Larry Mahan, picked up ten yards on an end-around. Cahill took the ball, dropped back, and threw a scoring strike to Daniel Bell, recently converted from quarterback to fullback, for the first touchdown. The left tackle Drury missed the extra point kick and the score stood in Leominster's favor 6–0. The second LHS score came in the third period. Leominster began its drive on its own forty-three-yard line after Amesbury's second-half kickoff. Hard runs by Danny Bell and Cahill culminated in two successive first downs. Cahill ran hard on a cutback over tackle and picked up twelve more yards. Caisse and Cahill alternated on eight-yard gains and Bell tore off ten more yards which gave Leominster a first down on the Amesbury five-yard line. Cahill netted two yards on the first play and Bell finished the drive on second down with a touchdown run. Cahill passed to Bell for the extra point and a LHS 13–0 lead.

The game was far from over. Leominster kicked off to Amesbury. The visitor's right halfback, Drew, returned the ball to his own forty. Amesbury quarterback Brozwick dropped back to pass. His left halfback Justin went up, snatched the pass, and cut toward the Leominster stands. A wall of Leominster defenders closed in as the crowd rose to its feet. Justin quickly reversed field and dashed across the gridiron. Only Joe Killelea was in a position to make the stop. Amesbury's talented left tackle Loeman had hustled downfield to throw a flying block.

---

119 *Leominster Enterprise,* October 29, 1931.

Killelea was cut off and Justin sidestepped into the end zone for an Amesbury touchdown. Justin's extra point kick was blocked by Wilson, Leominster's defensive lineman and center.

The fourth quarter featured aggressive Amesbury defense that pressured Cahill's pass attempts and played well against the run. Late in the final period, Amesbury's opportunity came. The visitors were forced to punt. Justin sent the ball high and deep into Leominster territory where Killelea waited. The Leominster quarterback failed to catch the ball cleanly and fumbled it away. Amesbury's Loeman recovered the fumble on the Leominster twenty. Amesbury attempted a trick play—a triple pass followed by a lateral—but the play failed when the runner tripped over his blocker. On the next play, Justin targeted his left end Robert George, but the end dropped the pass at the goal line. The Blue and White were courting disaster, but rose up to defend three successive passes, one stopped for a short gain, another batted down, and the final attempt incomplete.

The visitors got one more possession, this time starting at their own twenty-eight-yard line. With only seconds left, Justin fired successive desperate passes, all of which fell incomplete. LHS held on for an important win. The third win of 1933 extended the Leominster winning streak to thirteen games. More importantly, Broderick's team had been sorely tested for the first time that season and had come out on top. Despite the win, Broderick was not satisfied with his team's effort. He knew that the schedule would only become more difficult as the season progressed. The team would not have to wait long for its next big challenge.

The Blue and White had a short week before its fourth game, which was played at Doyle Field on Thursday, October 12, Columbus Day. Leominster hosted a powerful eleven from Chelsea High School for the holiday contest. As the football teams of Chelsea and Leominster were preparing to celebrate an explorer who reshaped the world, ominous events were brewing that would change history. German chancellor Adolf Hitler announced new foreign policies on October 14. Germany would immediately withdraw from the world disarmament conference, as well as the League of Nations, by 1935. A spokesman for the French government said the announcement was "the gravest news in twenty years." U.S. Secretary of State Gordon Hull and his department huddled to discuss the news and brief the president. Hitler took further dramatic action, dissolving the Reichstag, Germany's Parliament. A new election seating more members of the Nazi party would demonstrate the German people's endorsement of the new foreign policy. The gravity of these developments was not fully appreciated in the fall of 1933.[120]

Americans were already shaken by the collapse of their economy. Their capacity to digest additional calamities, especially those on the European continent, was limited. The *Sentinel* occupied itself tracking the number of persons receiving aid from the city welfare commission. The week ending October 7 saw a slight decrease in the number of citizens to whom food was distributed. Leominster assisted 447 residents at a per capita cost of ninety-four cents, down from 452 persons the week before.

It was a serious world and Americans thirsted for entertainment. Ten-cent movies, radio programming, and sports were welcome relief from everyday cares. Americans could "hear the world of sports" over a Philco radio. Philco print ads proclaimed "Give your home a REAL radio—a new Philco and enjoy reception of the big games of sportdom as if you were right on the sideline!" New models were available on "easiest terms—$22.50 and up, at Gamache Cyclery of West Fitchburg."[121]

The country was enchanted with football. Leominster rooters had faith in their team as the squad prepared for its next big test. Chelsea had defeated a well-regarded Nashua, New Hampshire team the Saturday before. The *Sentinel* noted "Chelsea's stock shot up last Saturday when they pinned an unexpected defeat onto Nashua High." Leominster fans were concerned that their standout halfback Ronnie Cahill was limping badly at practice. Danny Bell, who played his first game as fullback against Amesbury, was also ailing with a strained hamstring.

When the football game with Chelsea kicked off at Doyle Field, neither Cahill nor Bell were in the starting lineup. The pace of the game was torrid. Each team played hard-nosed defense. Chelsea safety Latanzi, who also led the team as quarterback, was a standout. "Biff" Wilson, a roving defensive lineman who was Leominster's center when the Blue and White were in possession of the pigskin, slashed through the Chelsea's line with devastating effectiveness. The crowd cheered

---

120 *Fitchburg Sentinel*, October 14, 1933.
121 *Fitchburg Sentinel*, November 7, 1933.

enthusiastically when Cahill and Bell entered the game in the second quarter. Even at that early point of the season, there was little doubt that Cahill was one of the state's best halfbacks. Bell was a consistent performer who ran hard. Despite the stars' arrival, the first half ended scoreless.

The second half was a different story. Chelsea's Crimson Horde wore down—they could not sustain the fine play that characterized the first half. Leominster scored first, breaking through from the Chelsea one-yard line. Alton Caisse, the right halfback, took a lateral from Killelea and plunged into the end zone. The Blue and White Warriors added a second touchdown on a forty-five-yard pass from Cahill to Alfred Caisse. The fleet right end—"the only 10.2 man on the field" according to the *Enterprise*—made a spectacular run after the catch.[122] The last touchdown of the day, which also belonged to the home team, came when Chelsea fumbled the ball on its own twenty. Leominster took advantage of the turnover and Cahill notched a second touchdown pass to Killelea on the very first play of the possession.

The final score was Leominster 20, Chelsea 0. With its fourteenth straight victory, Leominster was justifying the reputation already circulating in the Boston newspapers. The *Enterprise* noted that "Leominster has been nominated by the erstwhile indifferent Boston scribes as being one of the best teams of the state this year."[123] Unfortunately, the local press was also concerned about another reputation: the one belonging to some of the team's fans. The *Enterprise* warned:

> The gang from the city that congregates behind the bench at every football game and hoots and jeers at the visiting coach and players should be taken out beyond the 12 mile limit and dumped overboard. The vast majority of the Leominster people are sportsmen and like to treat visitors like (gentlemen). The Bowery talk, which is perpetuated by a few would be smart alecs, gives the city a black eye.[124]

---

122 *Leominster Enterprise,* October 13, 1933.
123 *Leominster Enterprise,* October 11, 1933.
124 *Leominster Enterprise,* October 6, 1933.

Some of Leominster's residents had other things on their mind that Columbus Day. The city's Italian population celebrated at Columbo Hall. Nine organizations were represented by the crowd of 350, who listened to an address by Judge Felix Forte of Boston. Forte, the Grand Venerable of the Massachusetts chapter of the Sons of Italy, told the assembled:

> This is not a local holiday. The discovery of America by the illustrious Genoan navigator is more a national event. I might say it's an international event, and should be celebrated by the entire western hemisphere. For after Columbus came all of the other navigators who opened the sea roads to this side of the earth. But still in this state we see business kept open, and the only Americans who devote any time are those who spring from the same race as Columbus.[125]

Leominster's only public observance of Columbus Day, the football game aside, was an exercise at the Lancaster Street School. The celebration was attended by parents, many of Italian heritage. The school's district encompassed Lincoln Terrace, where much of Leominster's Italian population lived. The event raised funds, which were used to purchase equipment for the school.[126]

Columbus Day and the Chelsea game faded. The Leominster gridders approached the halfway mark of their season and the team's first game away from Doyle Field. The Blue and White's next opponent was Rogers High School of Newport, Rhode Island. LHS practiced without Cahill, Bell, and Bernard Sweeney, a fullback who was injured in the Athol game on September 30. The players who were healthy were schooled in the Pop Warner system employed by Rogers High. In those days, long before the West Coast Offense or Tampa Two, teams often resorted to the Warner or Rockne systems. Leominster employed the latter, which was organized on the basis of deception first, then speed and power. The Warner system prioritized power, then speed and deception. Broderick readied his charges for both the trip and

---

125 *Leominster Enterprise,* October 16, 1933.
126 *Leominster Enterprise,* October 16, 1933.

the different offensive philosophy. The Leominster B-squad faithfully employed Rogers's plays in preparatory scrimmages.

The Blue and White Warriors arrived for the game on Saturday, October 21. The teams traded jabs and touchdowns during the first half which ended knotted at 6. Leominster's first-half score was made by fullback Deamicis, who was making his first start in place of Bell (Bell was converted to fullback from quarterback when Sweeney was hurt). Once again, Leominster, led by Cahill, outlasted the opposition in the second half. Cahill launched a number of brilliant passes, two that were good for touchdowns. Cahill ran for a touchdown, his third altogether, and Leominster defeated Rogers High 25–6.

Some of the visiting Leominster fans celebrated their team's fifteenth straight victory with little restraint. Reading between the lines of the *Enterprise*'s account of it all, the unbridled enthusiasm bordered on a riot. Nevertheless, sportswriter Bill Yeaw assigned some of the blame to Newport's finest:

> Of course all of the fault was not Leominster. The incident could have been averted if police officers had used more tact with Leominster people all around. The blue coats might have been able to have discerned that the goal posts were going down anyway. As a matter of fact, 2 or 3 officers were in favor of letting Leominster fans rip them up but whoever was in charge of the squad couldn't see it that way and he was all for keeping the 2x4's aloft. When he affirmed in sonorous tones that the posts were not going down, the crowd went haywire. The goal posts went down all right, but that was not enough. There were several imbeciles who had to add something to the celebration and that was when things were done that all sports fans of Leominster regret and cannot condone.[127]

Leominster's eleven and their rooters got a chance to test their traveling form again the following week. The Blue and White's next opponent was Framingham High School on Saturday, October 28. Bill Yeaw intoned to his *Enterprise* readers, "Dust off the old tin lizzie, put

---

127 *Leominster Enterprise*, October 25, 1933.

a bromo seltzer in the gasoline tank and let her explode, we are going to Framingham …"[128] Fitchburg had defeated Framingham 27–0 the previous Saturday. Followers of Leominster and Fitchburg were already sizing each other up in advance of the much-anticipated Thanksgiving meeting. Leominster's contest with Framingham was an opportunity for comparative measure. The Leominster result nearly matched the Fitchburg win over Framingham. In the words of the *Fitchburg Sentinel*, "The powerful Blue and White football machine of Leominster High crushed Framingham 26–0 … "[129] Cahill ran for a touchdown and passed for two more. One of the tosses was a forty-two-yard touchdown strike to Larry Mahan. The pass spiraled forty yards in the air and neatly met Mahan in stride. Killelea plunged in from the one-yard line for Leominster's last touchdown of the contest. The run was set up by a fifteen-yard scamper by Bernard Sweeney who made his first appearance at fullback since his September injury. Bell and Deamicis also saw duty; the Blue and White now had great depth at the fullback position. On the down side, standout center Biff Wilson was injured in the fourth quarter while recovering a fumble.

The post-game antics that started at Newport continued in the "Railroad City." The November 1 edition of the *Enterprise* was filled with reports of misdeeds connected with both the Framingham game as well as the annual Halloween visits from ghosts and tricksters. Halloween "daubing," the practice of marring windows with soap or wax, was in evidence throughout the city. Some of the windows were "decorated" with irregular markings, sometimes with obscenities or, in a few instances, the patriotic NRA letters. One home on Hall Street had its clothes line and its contents torn up. The home at 231 Merriam Avenue had a window broken. Street signs were stolen and rearranged to confuse those who might rely on the markers.[130]

The football vandals aroused the ire of Framingham school officials and caused the superintendent to write the *Enterprise*:

> There is no question about the overemphasis given to football in Leominster. Spring and late summer practices

---

128 *Leominster Enterprise,* October 27, 1933.
129 *Fitchburg Sentinel*, October 30, 1933.
130 *Leominster Enterprise*, November 1, 1933.

bring about that overemphasis and to a certain extent, develop the attitude so undesirable and so unworthy, which was here Saturday. The attitude has not been confined to the game or to their game in Newport last Saturday. As far as Leominster is concerned it will only be a matter of short time when they will find it very difficult to find schools who are willing to play them. No community intends to be subjected to Saturday, nor to insults and abuse when visiting in a town as guests.[131]

Some of the Blue and White followers had worn out their road welcome. Leominster had a bit of a gritty edge and a very good football team. Enthusiasm grew with each passing week and every new victory. It was fortuitous that Leominster returned home for its seventh game against Clinton. The friendly confines of Doyle Field were good medicine for the injured Blue and White Warriors.

For the first time since the Athol game, the squad had all of its starters available. Sweeney, who had been out the longest due to an arm injury, was effective. He scored two of Leominster's four touchdowns—all of the home team's six-pointers came on the ground that afternoon. Cahill crossed the goal line once. Another Leominster touchdown came under very unusual circumstances.

In the game's first period, Clinton found itself stalled deep in its own territory. Clinton quarterback Anastos waited for the long snap in his own end zone. Anastos handled the snap and despite pressure from the Leominster defense, got off a booming punt. At the very instant the pigskin reached its zenith, a sudden wind came up and stopped the ball's advance, blowing it back toward the Clinton goal. With the remarkable cooperation of the gust, the ball dropped in the Clinton end zone where it was pounced on by Leominster tackle Brooks.

Leominster converted three of its extra points, one the result of a Cahill rush and the other two on kicks by the newly healthy Sweeney. The Blue and White prevailed 27–0. The gallant gridders gained even more momentum, stretching their string of victories to seventeen. Many

---

131 *Leominster Enterprise,* November 1, 1933.

of those victories came at the expense of bigger football programs with strong reputations.

Leominster's eighth opponent of 1933 was not a power from the eastern part of the state of Massachusetts. In fact, Gardner High School was a smaller school a dozen miles to the west, but not one to be taken lightly. The Chair City had a long and rich football tradition. The young men from Gardner were always ready for a game with Leominster or Fitchburg regardless of the odds. Throughout a gridiron history with the aforementioned schools that dated to the nineteenth century, Gardner earned a number of great victories. Gardner enjoyed its own rivalry with both schools.

Leominster traveled to Gardner on Saturday, November 11 for its last road game of the season. Fans on both sides expected a tough game, but they may not have anticipated the drama that would unfold. Gardner coach Phillip Tarpey aligned his defense in a loose six-man front in order to provide extra protection against Cahill's passes. The strategy would pay dividends throughout the game as Gardner intercepted four passes in Leominster territory. Leominster's defense rose to the occasion and none of the interceptions resulted in points. Not all of Leominster's turnovers came through the air.

Gardner punted to Leominster early in the second period. Leominster started its drive on their own twenty-five-yard line. On the second play from scrimmage, Cahill fumbled the ball. Gardner's Michniewicz recovered the ball and provided his team another golden opportunity. On the first play of their revived possession, Gardner's left halfback Freeman was stopped by the Blue and White for no gain. On the next play, quarterback Crossley ran for a first down. Freeman readied himself, and his turn came again. The speedy halfback maneuvered through the left side of Leominster's line and dashed to the sideline. He fended off three would-be Blue and White tacklers with a straight arm and crossed the goal line. Freeman kicked the extra point.

Leominster was behind for the first time in their 1933 season. It was a stunning turn of events. The Gardner touchdown was only the third scored against Leominster in eight games. In the eighteen games since the beginning of the 1932 season through that November afternoon in the Chair City, the Blue and White had allowed a mere five touchdowns, one of which was scored by Concord High against the B-squad in a Leominster blowout. The only other score allowed in 1932 was also credited to Gardner. The Blue and White survived that game by a 14–6 tally.

In the 1933 contest, Leominster faced the real prospect of suffering its first defeat in almost two years at the hand of the plucky Wildcats. Leominster was held scoreless through the first three quarters of play. At one critical point in the third period, Gardner returned one of the Cahill interceptions to the Leominster seven-yard line. Leominster's defense fought with all the desperation dictated by the dire circumstances. The Blue and White held, and the Chair City eleven turned the ball over on downs.

The final period started with an exchange of punts. Gardner intercepted Cahill again, this time on the Leominster twenty-seven. The Blue and White stopped the first two Gardner runs, giving up only two yards. GHS took to the air on both third and fourth downs. Each time the ball fell incomplete. LHS had survived yet another potential disaster. The Blue and White took over on their own twenty-five. The offense finally began to click. Three runs and a short pass resulted in two first downs. Leominster advanced the ball to its forty-seven. Then Sweeney picked up twenty-eight yards on a brilliant run that established a new set of downs on the Chair City twenty-five. Caisse and Sweeney runs combined for another first down, but Mahan gave back ten yards on an end-around that Gardner smelled out. Less than two minutes remained on the clock.

Sweeney ran for three yards. On third down, Cahill rolled out wide, breaking hard for the sideline. The quarterback pulled up and cocked his arm, releasing a spiral that floated into Alfred Caisse's waiting hands as he crossed the Gardner goal line. There was little time left on the clock. Leominster's only hope rested on an extra point try. A successful conversion could not earn an eighteenth straight win but would preserve an undefeated season. Wilson snapped the ball back and Killelea got the ball down quickly. The Gardner stands roared loudly as Sweeney concentrated on his task. The fullback faced the most important place kick of his playing days. He kept his head down and made square contact with the ball. The kick sailed cleanly through the goal posts— Leominster had its tie. The game ended with a Leominster kickoff and two last Gardner runs. The Blue and White preserved its undefeated season, barely. The following week 1,300 intrepid fans braved wintry winds to watch the Blue and White prevail easily over Punchard High School of Andover at Doyle Field. Leominster posted forty-one points and held Punchard scoreless. Much of the game featured Leominster's underclassmen. Americo Spacciapoli relieved Cahill at left halfback and led Leominster with his arm and legs on a drive that culminated with a one-yard plunge by Deamicis. Spacciapoli, Rodriquenz (who substituted for right halfback Caisse), and Deamicis all added additional scores. Sophomore Mark K. O'Toole dominated on defense with a number of blistering tackles.[132] Leominster's domination was complete.

The Blue and White had one game left in 1933—Fitchburg. The 1933 Thanksgiving game was perhaps the most eagerly awaited in the long rivalry between the two schools. Leominster had but one blemish in its last nineteen contests: the tie with Gardner. That one footnote of imperfection would not be important if the Blue and White could achieve victory against Fitchburg.

If history and tradition were not enough, sportswriters across the state universally agreed that this Fitchburg-Leominster game would decide the unofficial state championship. Each team had compiled dazzling statistics over their respective undefeated seasons. Leominster outscored its opponents 237–19 in 1933. In the nineteen games prior to Thanksgiving 1933, the Blue and White outscored their foes 442-31 while notching eighteen victories and one tie. Fitchburg was equally

---

132 Mark K. O'Toole was the son of Mark L. O'Toole who played in the very first Leominster-Fitchburg game on October 20, 1894. Three successive generations followed Mark O'Toole onto the gridiron for Leominster High School. O'Toole's sons (David, class of 1931; Richard, class of 1933; and Mark, class of 1936) all played for Leominster. The youngest son, Mark K. O'Toole, an army air force lieutenant, was killed in action during World War II. The elder O'Toole's daughter, Jane, LHS class of 1943, married Dr. John J. Curley's son, John J. Curley, Jr., who played football for Leominster's graduating class of 1942. Two sons of John J Curley, Jr. played on the Leominster team: Michael, who graduated in 1973, and Daniel, who played on the Leominster undefeated team of 1974. Daniel graduated in 1977. Michael Curley's sons were fourth-generation Leominster football players, Mark O'Toole Curley graduated in 2002, and Michael graduated in 2007.

devastating. The Red and Gray put up 278 points to a meager 34 allowed during its unblemished first ten games of 1933.

When the rivals lined up at Doyle Field in 1933, it was the first Thanksgiving game at which both teams were undefeated—something that has not been repeated in the seventy-six years since. In a year of incredible change and challenge, the long football tradition of Leominster and Fitchburg contributed its own measure to the extraordinary times. The stage was set like never before.

—— Chapter 10: ——

Thanksgiving 1933

The Great Schoolboy Football teams collided at Doyle Field yesterday morning in a sensational and dramatic struggle for football supremacy before a vast and colorful throng of more than 10,000 spectators. Both teams were undefeated. Not only was victory at stake but also the rightful claim of the victors to the mythical schoolboy state Championship.

—Fitchburg Sentinel, December 1, 1933

The traditional Thanksgiving game between Fitchburg and Leominster high schools was never more hotly anticipated. The rivals had met in forty-nine games over the preceding thirty-nine years; not all of the games were played on Thanksgiving. During thirteen of the years from 1897 through 1904 and 1910 through 1916, the teams met twice. In 1900, 1902, and 1923 the teams didn't play each other.[133]

---

133 The teams didn't play in 1900 when Leominster sought a new opponent after the Fitchburg team was suspended for a low academic standing. The 1902 squads traded verbal barbs but never met on the gridiron, each claiming the other didn't want a game. The 1923 hiatus might be the most interesting of all. Fitchburg broke off athletic relations when

The 1933 edition of the Leominster-Fitchburg rivalry featured two of the greatest schoolboy football teams ever fielded in Massachusetts. Both of the teams were dominant. The last time Leominster had lost a game was on Thanksgiving Day 1931, the first Leominster-Fitchburg game played on Doyle Field.

The Fitchburg team possessed equally impressive statistics. No team had scored more than one touchdown against Fitchburg except Quincy High School in a contest won by the Red and Gray by a score of 21–13. That game, played November 18 in the mud and slush, had not been as close as the score indicated. Quincy registered both of its touchdowns on interceptions against Fitchburg's second team when the Red and Gray had the game in hand. Another twelve points scored against Fitchburg came in games that were routs.

Each team brought offensive firepower and a stout, proven defense. Their followers had a difficult time imagining that either could lose. Fans analyzed results achieved against common opponents. Sportswriters, local and Boston-based, hinted at the growing importance of the Thanksgiving game as Fitchburg and Leominster trimmed one eastern schoolboy powerhouse after another.

The game soon generated the sort of energy that quickly becomes contagious. The times were extraordinary, and in the midst of the Great Depression, the atmosphere surrounding the great rivalry was heightened all the more. Residents of the two cities and Americans everywhere were in need of something to feel good about. If the object of joy happened to be a time-honored tradition of great civic pride, even the better. Leominster-Fitchburg schoolboy football was more important than it had ever been.

Preparations were made for a record crowd. Leominster's police chief John B. Mead assigned thirty-two officers on foot and an additional ten motorcycle state policemen for crowd and traffic control. He also announced a rather interesting protocol, instructing his officers not to

---

a Leominster School official complained about a Fitchburg basketball player participating in a tournament at Tufts University in Boston since that player had punched out two teeth of a Leominster player on the court two weeks before. The Fitchburg school officials were indignant that the Leominster superintendent didn't understand the "one free slug per season rule" that was a feature of high school basketball of the time.

interfere with any attempt by the crowd to take down the goal posts after the game.[134]

The *Sentinel* predicted a record turnout. Seven thousand tickets, all of the available seating, were sold in advance. Thousands were expected to buy standing-room admittance. Each school conducted "rousing" pep rallies on the day before the game. The football teams made their final preparations, which were designed to keep the boys focused in the midst of all the hoopla. [135]

Leominster held a brief signal drill and then coach Broderick and his assistant Ted Kucharski took the team "far from the well meaning rooters."[136] The Blue and White squad returned to Leominster for an evening meal as guests of the Leominster Lodge of Elks at an undisclosed location. All of the pre-game activities were quite covert and calculated. The level of forethought certainly underscored that stakes were very high.

Fitchburg's final practice before the pivotal game was held on Tuesday, November 28. Coach Amiott addressed a crowd of twelve hundred students, teachers, and administrators. Amiott would not predict an outcome but instead chose to emphasize a pride in the school's sportsmanship.

> The sportsmanship of the school teams in the past 10 years has been beyond reproach. Our boys know how to conduct themselves. If the boys know how to conduct themselves, the student body will also do the same. Sportsmanship tomorrow, win or lose. The best rule of sportsmanship that I know is the golden rule—do unto others as you would have them do unto you. If you keep that in mind you'll be happy over your visit to Leominster.[137]

Amiott was well respected. His words to the student body bore testament to his widely held reputation as a gentleman. As far as the Fitchburg coach was concerned, his team's preparation for the

---

134 *Fitchburg Sentinel,* November 29, 1933.
135 *Fitchburg Sentinel,* November 29, 1933.
136 *Fitchburg Sentinel,* November 29, 1933.
137 *Fitchburg Sentinel,* November 29, 1933.

impending battle had begun the Thanksgiving before. The 1932 team left the gridiron " … and entered the locker room with tears in their eyes their bodies bruised and bumped." Fitchburg had fallen victim to the Blue and White by a score of 25–0 in 1932. It was the largest margin of victory Leominster had ever posted over Fitchburg, save the rivals' very first games of 1894, in which Leominster beat Fitchburg 40–0. The returning Red and Gray players had no intention of repeating the experience of the previous year. The Fitchburg boys felt confident that their cheeks would not be stained by tears when the final whistle sounded on Doyle Field in 1933.

Fans of both schools hoped for good weather. Each team had a high-powered offense led by a triple-threat star, Cahill for Leominster and Mackie for Fitchburg. The rooters wanted to see their offenses play at their best, without the deterrence of poor weather.

Thanksgiving Day dawned under clear skies. The weather was ideal and the record crowd filed into Doyle Field. Fans sported their school colors. Fitchburg clothier Kimball and Son Co. advertised a special in its store window before the game. The Fitchburg faithful could purchase a red and gray handkerchief and football pin for twenty-five cents. The grandstand on the southern side of the field was draped in red and gray. Across the way, the Leominster fans made their presence known, draped in the blue and white of their football Warriors.

Bill Mackie rose early on Thanksgiving morning. His walk to Crocker Field to meet the team bus for the trip to Leominster felt different from any of the ten prior game days that season. On that day, Mackie had an escort meet him at his Lawrence Street home for the two-mile walk. For safety's sake, Fitchburg's talented halfback was accompanied by Ed Sullivan, captain of a Fitchburg squad in the 1920s. Quarterback Cahill lived on Grand Street, one of the streets that bordered Doyle Field. He did not have far to walk.

Both teams arrived to a measure of pageantry. Leominster did not have a high school band in 1933. A local contingent of Girl Scouts fielded a fife and drum corps which provided a punctuation to the cheers from the Leominster side. The Red and Gray rooters were led onto Doyle Field by a well-drilled marching band under the direction of J. Edward Bouvier.

The game officials were a hand-picked quartet: James E. Keegan, referee, of Pittsfield; A. R. Dorman, umpire, of New Bedford, a Columbia alum; Harold R. Goewey, backfield judge, of Pittsfield, a Syracuse alum; and Percy R Carpenter, head linesman, of Worcester, a Harvard graduate. These men had officiated some of the most important college games of the season. Followers of both teams were confident and honored to have such a heralded group on hand for the paramount game of the Massachusetts schoolboy season.[138]

The officials gathered with the captains at midfield for the coin toss. The Leominster team was represented by Cahill and Biff Wilson. The Red and Gray were led by the Esielionis brothers, Stanley and Felix, who were elected co-captains at the disappointing conclusion of the prior season. Fitchburg, touted by many as the favorite, won the toss and elected to receive.

Cahill got things started, booting the ball into the clear November sky. Mologhan waited anxiously as the pigskin sailed in his direction. The right halfback caught the ball cleanly on the twenty-yard line and returned the ball to the twenty-six. Cahill made the tackle.

Fitchburg could not gain a first down on its initial possession. Leominster's defenders forced Mackie to sweep wide and the talented back could not turn the corner on either first or third down. Mackie punted to his counterpart. Cahill returned the ball ten yards to the Leominster thirty-one-yard line where the Blue and White began their first possession of the game.

Cahill crashed the line and picked up a hard-fought five yards. Alton Caisse was stopped at the line of scrimmage on second down. The home team got set for third down. The backfield shifted right and the long snap went directly to Caisse. Caisse swept and Cahill took the ball on a reverse. Fitchburg's Brodeur reached the Leominster back five yards past the line, but Cahill escaped the would-be tackle and dashed another ten yards to midfield as the Leominster crowd roared its approval. Fitchburg stopped Cahill on first down but Caisse picked up six yards on the next try. On the next play, Cahill swept and made a cut back to the center of the field. The Leominster faithful rose to their feet as their hopes for a breakaway ignited with a sensational move. Chalmers made a saving tackle at the Fitchburg twenty-three-yard line. The Leominster offense

---

138 *Fitchburg Sentinel,* November 29, 1933.

was on the move and the crowd hurrahed in approval. The cheers abated briefly as the Red and Gray stopped another Cahill reverse. The noise reached another crescendo as Cahill swept to the Fitchburg ten on a lateral from quarterback Daniel Bell.

The Leominster fans were frenzied by the early scoring opportunity. The Red and Gray rooters chanted for their defense to hold. Twice the Fitchburg cheers were rewarded as the visitor's defense stopped Leominster runs. On third down, Cahill swept while searching for a target in the end zone. He lofted a pass which fell incomplete in the Fitchburg goal. The drive failed and the Fitchburg fans were relieved. Fitchburg, in accordance with the rules of the day, took over on its own twenty because of the incompletion in the end zone.

Fitchburg managed two first downs but the drive stalled when the third series of downs lost yardage. On fourth down Mackie dropped back to punt. But the Red and Gray gambled. After taking the long snap, the southpaw passer cocked his arm and sent an aerial downfield that fell incomplete. Fitchburg fans braced as opportunity knocked once again for the Blue and White.

Leominster took over on the Fitchburg thirty-yard line. On first down, Cahill forced a pass to his intended target, Caisse, which Aaron Keto nearly intercepted. On the next play, Cahill took the ball on a reverse, a staple play of the Rockne (or Notre Dame) system that coach Broderick employed. Leominster was unlucky this time, losing the ball. Russell Dik, the Fitchburg center/defensive lineman, and Lauri Shattuck combined to make a jarring tackle and Cahill fumbled. James Leo recovered for the Red and Gray and another threat was averted as the first period expired.

Fitchburg opened the second stanza on its own thirty-four. Mackie was stopped by Wilson and Cahill on first down but Mackie then connected with fullback Shattuck, who replaced Raoul Brodeur, who was injured earlier in the game, on a twenty-yard toss over the sophomore's shoulder. Shattuck started down the Leominster sideline and broke the tackle of Danny Bell. James Leo threw a timely downfield block clearing the last Leominster defender and Shattuck rolled into the end zone for the game's first score. Mackie successfully booted the try after and the Red and Gray took a 7–0 lead.

Mackie kicked to Cahill who fielded the ball cleanly on the eighteen-yard line and returned it to the thirty where Stanley Esielionis made the stop. Leominster sustained a drive which included a twenty-four-yard pass by Cahill to Wilfred DeBellefeuville. But once again the Blue and White Warriors stalled, this time on the Fitchburg thirty-six-yard line, where the Red and Gray took over.

The teams exchanged possessions and Fitchburg's offense produced a threat, earning a first down on the Leominster thirty-yard line. Cahill made a hard tackle on the visitor's first try but got a cleat in the face. Leominster's star suffered a cut eyelid and had to leave the field. Under the rules in effect, Cahill could not return to the field of play until the beginning of the third quarter. Cahill's replacement was sophomore Americo Spacciapoli, or "Spacci" for short. It didn't take the understudy long to make a mark. Spacciapoli made a blistering tackle on second down holding Fitchburg to no gain. A Mackie pass fell incomplete on the next play. On fourth down, Mackie dropped back. The Leominster defense teed off on what was sure to be a pass. The trio of Nunios Papaz, Danny Bell, and Larry Brooks sacked Mackie and ended the Fitchburg threat. Neither team could develop any rhythm on offense after Fitchburg was halted. The half ended with Fitchburg holding a 7–0 advantage.

The two squads retreated to the field house for a few moments' rest and halftime instruction. The game had developed into a classic battle and each team had played a very physical half of football. Leominster players could take some solace in their offensive production. The difference in the game was Mackie's long pass and Shattuck's brilliant run. The Red and Gray owned the only big play of the first half. Exactly what the respective coaches told their charges at the half was not recorded. Broderick reassured his boys that they were in the game. Amiott reminded his players that they had not earned anything yet. Two crucial quarters of a remarkable season of football remained. Like an evenly matched heavyweight bout, the remaining minutes promised to be a slugfest.

The second half started with Mackie's squibbed kickoff bounding down the field. The poor kick had unintended results. Cahill and Bell both moved to field the pigskin as it took an irregular path. Bell touched it but couldn't maintain control and Stanley Esielionis crashed through to recover the ball on the Leominster thirty-two-yard line.

The Blue and White faced critical circumstances—their visitors had a big opportunity. Mackie went over guard for four yards. Shattuck picked up another four yards over center and Mackie swept for two yards and a first down at the Leominster twenty-two. Then Shattuck was stopped by Papaz, Cahill, Wilson, and Sweeney. Stanley Esielionis opened a gaping hole on the right side and Mackie churned out thirteen yards for a first down on Leominster's nine-yard line. Shattuck and Mackie combined on two carries, which set up the Red and Gray on the two. Mackie tested the Leominster line once more, who stopped the half back just a half yard from the goal line. The stage was set for the most critical of fourth-down plays. Mackie cracked the line between his center Russell Dik and his right guard Aaron Keto. Dik and Keto strained against the Leominster defense and surged just enough to permit Mackie a path to the end zone. The snap for the try after was bad and the holder James Chalmers tried to salvage the point on a pass, but the ball sailed wide. Fitchburg held a 13–0 lead and the Blue and White were in a position that they had not faced in nineteen prior games.

The Blue and White had not trailed by two touchdowns since Thanksgiving 1931. The LHS squad was tested and the challenge was big. Mario Deamicis awaited Mackie's kick feeling the resolve shared by all of his teammates. The sophomore caught the kick and returned the ball fourteen yards to the Leominster forty-four. The Fitchburg defense repulsed two Leominster runs. On the third down, Cahill pulled up and fired a pass to DeBellefeuville which was good for twenty-seven yards. Leominster was set up on the Fitchburg thirty-seven.

Cahill bulled his way for five yards to the thirty-two where Dik made the stop. Deamicis was held to no gain. Cahill took the third-down snap sweeping right and running hard for twenty yards. Leominster had a first down on the Fitchburg twelve and a new sense of vigor. Sophomore Frank Rodriguenz picked up five yards. Cahill smashed through the Fitchburg line on the next play. The halfback twisted and squirmed for six yards and Dik saved the score, stopping Cahill at the one-yard line. Dik was knocked unconscious in the process. Cahill scored on the very next play but missed the extra point. Leominster was back in the game, trailing the Red and Gray 13–6.

Mackie took Cahill's kick thirteen yards to the Fitchburg thirty-eight-yard line. The Red and Gray moved the ball forty-two yards on Mackie's powerful running behind the solid blocks of the Esielionis brothers. When the third period ended, Fitchburg was poised to add to its lead, having driven to the Leominster twenty-yard line.

Mackie opened the final period with runs for three and six yards which resulted in a first down at the Leominster ten. Shattuck picked up four more yards. Larry Brooks stopped Mackie cold. Fitchburg struck again on the next play as Chalmers flipped a lateral to Mackie as he was being tackled. Mackie picked up blocks from Mologhan, Shattuck, and Stanley Esielionis on his was to pay dirt. Both teams were offside on the try after goal and when the play was repeated, Shattuck carried the ball for an extra point. Fitchburg lead 20–6.

Mackie boomed the ensuing kickoff into the Leominster end zone for a touchback. Leominster converted one first down but the second series ended with a Cahill punt, one of only four punts made by both teams in the entire contest. Fitchburg could not manage a first down in its next possession as the Leominster defense stiffened, realizing the growing crisis they faced. Leominster obtained good field position at its own forty-two-yard line, a Mackie punt netting only eleven yards.

Leominster drove the ball on the strength of Cahill's rushing to the Fitchburg one-yard line. Unfortunately for the Blue and White, they turned the ball over on downs tantalizingly close to the much-needed score. But sometimes football fortunes shift faster than a blink of an eye. That was the case in the dramatic fourth quarter of the 1933 Thanksgiving game. On the very first Fitchburg play, Shattuck fumbled and the ever-alert Larry Mahan recovered the ball to the thundering approval of the home crowd. Fitchburg kept Rodriguenz out of the end zone on first down but could not deny Cahill on the next try. Cahill missed a critical try after. The errant kick was especially damaging given the lack of a two-point conversion in 1933.

The score stood Fitchburg 20, Leominster 12 with a rapidly expiring clock. After Cahill kicked off, Fitchburg picked up a first down, which assured victory. Leominster never regained possession. The seconds ticked off and the final whistle sounded.

It was a game that one team had to lose. While hard-fought losses carry a certain amount of respect and coaches rationalize about effort being paramount to result, those clichés often clang with a hollow reverberation in quiet locker rooms. Thanksgiving Day 1933 was distinct, not solely for the level of effort exerted by the losers, but also for the style of play. The entire game was devoid of a foul penalty (personal foul), this despite high emotions and the most physical of play. Sportsmanship, in the truest sense, accompanied every play from the opening kick through the final tick of the game clock. Bill Yeaw of the *Leominster Enterprise* defined the real lesson of football: "Play the best you know how, observe the rules and fight clean."[139]

The ancient rivals had played their most dramatic of contests in 1933. Each squad had given their city a season of pride, belonging, and hope. When the undefeated titans met, the boys left behind not only a score but also an untarnished example of giving their best effort when the stakes where highest.

Before one down of game was played, the *Enterprise* had suggested in the very first words of the pre-game coverage, "Reserve a niche in Leominster's Hall of Fame for the 1933 Football team." Both teams earned their distinction, and both will forever be remembered when those who cherish the game consider not only talent but character. Yeaw commenced his post-game coverage:

> Never has a team in a time of victory covered itself in more honor or distinction than did the Broderick coached charges yesterday and the fact they were on the short end of the score does not detract from the glory of their red blooded struggle.[140]

The Red and Gray concluded their first undefeated season and claimed the unofficial state championship. Gracious winners, the team reflected the leadership of their head coach. Principal Chalmers ruled out a playoff game with Lawrence High School. There was simply nothing more to prove, and Thanksgiving was a natural conclusion to the season. A few more dollars for the school were not a consideration. The victors were treated to a trip to New York City by boat. Bill Mackie still recalls the passage through the Cape Code Canal and the arrival in New York.

---

139 *Leominster Enterprise*, December 1, 1933.
140 *Leominster Enterprise*, December 1, 1933.

When the legendary, magical 1933 season concluded, it was Leominster's turn to wax philosophical:

> There is always the forward look, the hope that springs eternal, that other days are ahead, other Thanksgivings, other teams to match their wits and their muscles with the best Fitchburg can produce. Predictions are rash for none can foretell—hence the unstifled hope.[141]

---

141 *Leominster Enterprise*, December 1, 1933.

—— *Chapter 11:* ——

Humble Leaders

Blocking is the toughest job on a football field and you get ... absolutely no pats on the back, no headlines.

—Harold "Red" Grange, October 1924

The Great Depression was characterized by a lack of faith in the institutions of the American economy. Folks of all ages needed something or someone to believe in. The young men who took to the football field in 1933 grew up with the example of Red Grange. It was an age when boys believed in heroes, and those luminaries were more important than ever in 1933. Fitchburg's Mackie, Leominster's Cahill, and their respective teams sought to emulate players like Grange. By doing so they stirred hope for not only athletic achievement, but also for their communities. Cities and towns across America yearned for a better future during those difficult days. In doing so, they looked to the past. Traditions built upon solid values were a tonic to Depression-weary souls. A twenty-five-cent ticket for a football game was an admission to possibility. The play on the gridiron produced champions, acts of valor, and most importantly, young men who put their team first. It was an expression of just what the nation needed.

When Bill Mackie and Ronnie Cahill were barely ten years old, Red Grange prowled the college gridiron and prepared to launch his professional career. Remarkably, Grange played out the 1925 college football season for the University of Illinois Illini and just ten days later debuted as a member of the Chicago Bears. Grange wore the Bears' uniform for the very first time on Thanksgiving Day 1925. A record crowd of thirty-six thousand packed Wrigley Field to see the sensation of college football.

Grange was already an icon. His reputation was carved by sportswriters whose own notoriety was magnified by the greatness of their subject. Grantland Rice gave "the Illini Flash," an early Grange moniker, his permanent nickname. It is a long-held misconception that Rice christened Grange the "Galloping Ghost" after watching him lead Illinois to a win over mighty Michigan on October 18, 1924. That day witnessed a performance that helped establish Grange's singular place in the football world. Grange scored five touchdowns—four rushing, one passing. He ran for 212 yards, passed for 64 and ran back kickoffs for 126 more. Four of the touchdowns came in the first twelve minutes. It was powerful Michigan's first loss in twenty games. Despite all of that, it was not the performance that inspired the legendary title "Galloping Ghost."

While Grange was leading the Illini to a 39-14 win over Michigan, Rice was covering a contest between Army and Notre Dame. Observations made that Saturday gave rise to another piece of epic sports prose:

> Outlined against a blue-gray October sky, the four horsemen rode again. In dramatic lore they were known as famine, pestilence, destruction and death. These are only aliases. Their real names are Stuhldreher, Miller, Crowley and Layden.[142]

Just three weeks later, Rice took up his pen and jotted some of the sporting world's greatest imagery. The reporter had just witnessed Grange's courageous performance in a contest pitting the Illini against the Alonzo Stagg-coached University of Chicago. It was a gut-wrenching, hard-fought game. Grange kept his team in the fight. He was carried

---

142 Poole, *The Galloping Ghost: Red Grange*, 41.

from the field, but not in victory. The game ended in a tie. Grange passed out. Near the end of the game he fell face down, the result of a concussion and sheer exhaustion. Rice was moved to write:

> A streak of fire, a breath of flame,
> Eluding all who reach and clutch;
> A gray ghost thrown into the game
> That rival hands may never touch;
> A rubber bounding, blasting soul,
> Whose destination is the goal-
> Red Grange of Illinois.[143]

Professional football did not make Red Grange. The Galloping Ghost was a football legend before playing a single down for the Chicago Bears. But professional football awaited Grange nevertheless, and the pro sport was changed forever when he stepped onto the stage. The Bears and teams eager to host them were poised to fill seats with fans awaiting a chance to witness the exploits of the talented halfback.

Grange's football earnings totaled eight-two thousand dollars before his professional career was two weeks old.[144] His agent, Charles Pyle, who received one-half of Grange's earnings for his part, arranged another one hundred thousand dollars in endorsements. The money was breathtaking.

Grange became an instant member of a pantheon of sports figures, all legends of the 1920s. He joined boxing's Jack Dempsey, golf's Bobby Jones, and Babe Ruth as athletes who not only excelled but helped define their sport for future generations. To put Grange's earnings in perspective, none of Ruth's contracts with the Yankees ever exceeded eighty thousand dollars per year. Ruth played for fifty-two thousand dollars annually in the five seasons between 1922 and 1926.[145] The following year, the slugger signed a three-year contract for seventy thousand dollars per season and in 1930, he bargained hard for eighty-five thousand dollars, but signed for two years at eighty thousand

---

143 Poole, *The Galloping Ghost: Red Grange*, 62.
144 Poole, *The Galloping Ghost: Red Grange*, 171.
145 Montville, *The Big Bam: The Life and Times of Babe Ruth*, 247.

dollars per season.[146] More than 70 percent of the five million U.S. taxpayers who filed returns in 1921 did not report earnings exceeding four thousand dollars per year.

Despite a new-found wealth and celebrity that continued to grow, Grange retained a sense of humility. Grange grew upon in Wheaton, Illinois. He and his dad moved from Pennsylvania after his mother died while Grange was just a boy of five. His father persuaded him to go to college and his fraternity brothers urged him to play football for Illinois. Grange earned his own way as a collegian. He received no scholarship but instead lugged ice blocks, stocking the ice boxes of homes throughout Wheaton. Early in his college football career, he was dubbed the "Wheaton Iceman."

Teammates described Red Grange in a single word—humble. In recounting his gridiron accomplishments, Grange said:

> They built my accomplishments way out of proportion. I never got the idea that I was a tremendous big shot. I could carry a football well, but there are a lot of doctors and teachers and engineers who could do their thing better than I.[147]

When Grange died in 1991, one of his former Illini teammates confirmed the lasting reputation of the man behind the headlines.

> I'll use just one word—humble ... the most humble person I ever met. He'd make you feel at home, no matter who you were and he never bragged. Even the second string guys admired him. He'd tell them a tackle they made was the difference in the game.[148]

His talent was universally acclaimed. But Grange's stature was enhanced by a self-contained, unassuming perspective. Players like Grange meld with their teams in the most effective way. Contributions to a common purpose are magnified on the gridiron with electrifying

---

146 A 1933 contract resulted in the slugger taking a pay cut of twenty-three thousand dollars due to the Depression and his age. Montville, *The Big Bam: The Life and Times of Babe Ruth*, 298-299.

147 http://espn.go.com/classic/biography/s/Grange_Red.html.

148 *Chicago Daily Herald*, January 29, 1991.

results. The prospects of a team consisting of players dedicated to each other and led by humble example are never poor.

The young men who played high school football in 1933 grew up during the days Grange played professional football. Ronnie Cahill and Bill Mackie had a fine example in Red Grange, and they succeeded in emulating his humble leadership. Bill Mackie is a modest man. Today he observes football from a different perspective than most fans. Today's football is extremely celebratory. Players revel in individual feats, whether the achievement is a touchdown, pass reception, or a tackle. Mackie makes a simple but telling point: "I couldn't play the game by myself." When asked if he ever paused to celebrate a touchdown, Mackie quickly responds: "I didn't have time. I was more concerned about helping up the other ten guys that made the play succeed."

Bill Mackie and his team both set a Massachusetts scoring record in 1933. Sixty-two years later, Mackie received a telephone call from a reporter. Bill Gilman, a sportswriter for the *Fitchburg Sentinel,* wanted to know what Mackie thought about the impending fall of his scoring record at Fitchburg High School. "What record?" was his quick response. Mackie didn't know for one day of the prior six plus decades that he held the Fitchburg High School scoring mark. Rick Morales went on to set the new record on Thanksgiving Day of 1995. Bill was happy to surrender the record even if he held it consciously for just hours.

In 1990, Red Grange yielded his sixty-six-year-old touchdown record at Illinois. Howard Griffith, the new custodian of the Illini mark for single game, season, and career touchdowns, got a chance of a lifetime to meet the legend. Griffith was speechless.

> He said he was thrilled to meet me and I was saying to myself: this guy has done everything and I've done just a few things in college. To meet him and come back and share the experience with my teammates was tremendous.[149]

Mackie, like the man he regarded as a boy, was not focused on individual accolades. Their motivation came from relationships. They lived to support their teams and enjoy the people near them. In 1978, Grange visited his hometown. Wheaton turned out with awards and

---

149 *Associated Press,* January 29, 1991.

honors. When it was time to leave, Red gave all the memorabilia to D. Ray Wilson, the publisher of *Wheaton's Daily Journal*. He told Wilson to keep the items for the town's archive. He left with only one memento, a note from an elementary school girl who wrote "I love you Red."[150]

Bill Mackie settled into a career at the Norton Company of Worcester, Massachusetts, shortly after leaving high school in 1933. Mackie enjoyed seventy-five years of marriage with his late wife, Mary Julia, who passed away in 2009. The couple wed in 1934, just a year after Bill left high school. Bill and M. Julia, as she preferred to be called, were proud parents of a son, William Mackie, Jr. The younger Mackie and five grandchildren all possess a good measure of their father's and grandfather's athletic talent.

Today, Bill Mackie remains as modest as ever about the year he electrified Crocker Field and treated Fitchburg fans to a series of superb performances at a time when joy was sorely needed. As far as Bill Mackie is concerned, he was just one cog. He was a happy part of a big family that entered each contest with mutual respect and a simple goal: to do their job. Red Grange was no less modest, and no less willing to credit his coach or teammates. Regarding perhaps his most memorable football achievement, the five-touchdown performance that powered Illinois over Michigan in 1924, Grange was wholly unpretentious:

> (Coach Bob) Zuppke planned that game so carefully. I'm convinced that there isn't a team in the country that could've beaten us that day. Maybe the day before or the day after, but not that day. If Zuppke had called on the other halfback he could've done it. Your grandmother could've done it. I know my grandmother could have.[151]

The young men who played schoolboy football in 1933 had a valuable boyhood role model in the Galloping Ghost. Mackie's exemplary play, enhanced by genuine humility, was matched by Leominster's Ronnie Cahill. It is noteworthy that these young men roamed the gridiron at the same time, perhaps an underappreciated point of local history. Neither of the men ever viewed each other as counterparts. Success was

---

150 *Kokomo* (Indiana) *Tribune*, January 29, 1991.
151 *Chicago Daily Herald*, January 29, 1991.

not about Mackie and Cahill or a competition for individual honors. Both led their teams, not by their exploits, but by a deep and mutual respect for their teammates.

Ronnie Cahill played hard. He was a true competitor. It was a little difficult to reconcile his hard-nosed style of play with the calm demeanor he demonstrated off the field. Contemporaries convey the idea that the triple threat never thought very much of his own talents or got all that excited about an impending contest. He simply went out and took care of business on the field. Ronnie was an avid hunter. He enjoyed the solitude of a morning in the field. A dawn hunt on Thanksgiving Day 1932 gave rise to one of Leominster's most enduring football tales. That morning, the lure of a rural quarry caused Cahill to lose track of time. To the dismay of coach Broderick, his halfback was late for the team bus to the much-anticipated contest with rival Fitchburg. Even if tardy, Cahill was certainly not overawed by the impending big game, a match in which he helped lead Leominster to a 25–0 win and an undefeated season.

Those who knew Cahill and those who played with him all recall one essential thing: he never boasted about his football talent. More than that, he never talked about his football career unless asked. In his last years, Cahill resided with his daughter, Sandra and her husband, Jerry Belliveau. Jerry remembers his father-in-law as a quiet, unassuming man who lived for his family. When the two men were watching a televised football game, it was never apparent that the elder had had any special background on the gridiron. If Jerry inquired about Ronnie's football memories, Ronnie would politely answer—but never say more than what was necessary. On one occasion, when Jerry asked Ronnie if he ever played in a college All-Star Game, his father-in-law replied "yes." That was it, no additional color or recollections, just a simple affirmative. Ronnie Cahill played in the Eastern College All-Star Game against the NFL's New York Giants in 1940. Cahill helped lead the college team to a sensational win over the NFL champion Giants by a score of 16–7. The talented passer connected on eleven straight passes, part of an aerial barrage that felled the mighty Giants. Even in the quiet of the family parlor, more than five decades later, there wasn't the slightest boast or reminiscence, just a simple unpretentious nod.

Cahill and Mackie were young men with God-given talents. They each applied their gifts in the most dignified of ways and made their teams better for it. During some of America's darkest days, those young football players not only led their teams to success, but brightened their communities when folks needed that most. The nadir of the Great Depression was an extraordinary time that tested every American institution and the nation's very way of life. Football not only survived with the country but in many ways made those trying days just a little easier to survive.

A century from now or more, 1933 will be an even fainter memory. America will inevitably face challenges yet to be imagined. When those days come, the shining example of these athletes who took to the gridiron in that pivotal year will be as important as ever, if folks will simply pause and remember.

Afterword

The setting at Comiskey Park evoked all the imagery of Grantland Rice's Four Horsemen, save the blue-gray October sky. The dire portrait drawn by Rice did at least approximate the conditions as the NFL's two Chicago franchises met on the gridiron Sunday, November 28, 1943. The sky was overcast and the field was whipped by bitterly cold winds. Gusts blew snow squalls over the frozen turf.

The rosters of both the Bears and Cardinals were greatly depleted by the loss of players called into military service. Teams recruited players young and old to replace the departed veterans. Bears owner George Halas, himself a lieutenant commander stationed with the Seventh Fleet in the south Pacific, negotiated a contract from afar with Bronko Nagurski. The aging legend had been out of football since 1937. He ignored a body wracked by arthritis and injuries suffered in a wrestling career that continued after he left football. He returned to the Bears in 1943. He needed the five-thousand-dollar contract, and the Bears needed him.

Two other players, much younger than Nagurski, were ailing also. One of those players, Sid Luckman, the Bears' quarterback, was recovering from the flu. He was hospitalized just two days before the game.[152] Luckman graduated from Columbia in 1939 where he was coached by Lou Little. Luckman was catapulted to professional prominence leading the T–formation offense. Little, a Leominster

---

152 *Lowell Sun*, November 29, 1943.

native, had had his eye on another talented passer in the late 1930s, one with a hometown connection.

Ronnie Cahill, despite attending prep school in the same Manhattan neighborhood as Columbia, evaded Little's recruiting efforts and enrolled at Holy Cross, where he starred for the Crusaders from 1937 to 1939. Luckman was more than ample consolation for Little. The talented quarterback made a great contribution to Columbia's football program and polled third in the Heisman Trophy balloting in 1938. Luckman's professional performance in 1943 earned him the NFL's most valuable player award.[153] Cahill, a rookie that year, was the Cardinals' leading passer, completing 50 of his 109 attempts for 608 yards.[154] Cahill was not feeling well during the game with the Bears.

A season of pro football and the bone-chilling cold of Chicago's early winter were taking their toll. By the Thursday following the game against the Bears, Cahill was admitted to Leominster Hospital with a suspected case of pneumonia.[155] The Cardinals were counting on their rookie passer in their contest against the Bears. The team's line was crippled by injuries and the running attack was compromised.[156]

The two Chicago elevens were heading in opposite directions. The Bears entered the fray with a record of 7-1-1. The Cardinals were winless in nine games. The Bears were playing for the Western Division title and a championship game with the Washington Redskins. The Cardinals were playing for pride. The Green Bay Packers were right on the Bears' heels; a loss to the Cardinals would force a Bears-Packers playoff for the western title. The Bears were a heavy favorite as they took to Comiskey Field to face their cross-town foes.

Two men stood on the rock-hard turf. Each player had an important memory, each almost exactly a decade old. Nagurski led the Bears to the NFL's first championship ten years before on Wrigley Field. It was a memorable day in his football life. Ten years before, and far away from Chicago, Ronnie Cahill played the last game of an illustrious schoolboy football career. Cahill paced Leominster High School on Thanksgiving Day 1933, but his heroic efforts did not produce a win. It

---

153 Treat, *The Encyclopedia of Professional Football 6th Edition*, 370.
154 http://www.pro-football-reference.com/players/c/cahiron20-html.
155 *Berkshire East*, December 3, 1943.
156 *Wisconsin State Journal*, November 28, 1943.

was Leominster's first loss in two years. Cahill's efforts, even in defeat, brought a level of praise usually reserved for victors:

> Ronnie Cahill's work will long linger in memory. He will be remembered as one of the best backs that ever played for Leominster. His mighty work yesterday, sometimes without interference, sometimes with splendid interference, will take its place with stellar accomplishments of other Leominster heroes of the gridiron.[157]

Ronnie Cahill could have never imagined he would someday stand opposite the great Bronko Nagurski on a Chicago gridiron when he was suiting up for his last high school game. For that matter, Nagurski didn't figure on coming back to the game six years after his retirement. The Cardinals surprised the Bears that afternoon, leading 24–14 after three quarters of play. The unthinkable began to creep into the hearts of the Bears' fans.

The Bears' coach, "Hunk" Anderson, filling in for Halas, needed to make a move. With the start of the fourth quarter, he sent Nagurski in at fullback. More than forty thousand fans began a collective chant of "Bronko, Bronko, Bronko!"[158] The Cardinals' Chet Bulger yelled, "You're nothing but a goddamned old man."[159] Nagurski remembered another old man, Red Grange, who helped the Bears win a championship with a saving tackle in the 1933 championship. Nagurski summoned all of the strength left in his paunchy old frame and toted the leather seven times for fifty-four yards, the last carry a one-yard plunge that resulted in a Bears' touchdown. The Cardinals' lead was narrowed to three. Nagurski bulled for more yards in the next drive. A Luckman fake to the powerful fullback froze the defense enabling the quarterback to loft a twenty-five-yard pass to wingback Harry Clark who scored easily, giving the Bears a lead they would not surrender.

The Cardinals completed a winless season and the Bears went onto a championship win against the Redskins. Led by Luckman's record

---

157 *Leominster Enterprise,* December 1, 1933.
158 Dent, *Monster of the Midway,* 275.
159 Dent, *Monster of the Midway,* 276

five touchdown passes, the Bears outscored the Redskins 41–21.[160] Bronko Nagurski took satisfaction in his decision to come back—it was a good curtain call. If Cahill saw action in the Cardinals' last game, it was minimal. Despite ranking as high as fourth in the league passing, he did not figure in the scoring against the Bears.[161] Given his hospitalization just days later, he could not have been in top form. It was Ronnie Cahill's last game in the NFL. Within days of his hospital stay, Cahill was back in the woods enjoying the solitude of a hunt. The newspaper reported his health rebound when it noted he bagged a buck in Warwick, Massachusetts, a week after leaving the hospital.

The talented halfback had completed his professional playing days. He would soon trade his cleats for an enlistment in the Marine Corps. The quiet moments in the woods that December must have provided an opportunity for reflection. The football field had brought him success, though he never bragged about it. Contrasted against great accomplishments were pivotal losses. Beyond the Cardinals' dismal 1943 season and the Thanksgiving loss to Fitchburg in 1933, there was also a defeat at the hands of Boston College in his last game for the Crusaders of Holy Cross.

Cahill and the Crusaders had battled Boston College before a crowd of forty thousand at Fenway Park in November 1939.[162] Even in losing efforts, he never stopped trying. When the intrepid halfback left the playing field, a genuine ovation arose with equal force from both sides of the field. The challenges of 1933 left an indelible mark on Cahill, Mackie, and other young men of the gridiron—apply your talents, do so with humility and never give up.

---

160 Treat, *The Encyclopedia of Football (6ᵗʰ Edition)*, 89.
161 *Berkshire Eagle,* November 18, 1943.
162 *Leominster Enterprise,* July 30, 1965.

TABLE OF GAMES
1893 to 2009

Year	Winner	Score		Year	Winner	Score
1893	Leominster	8–6	*	1918	Fitchburg	20–0
1894	Leominster	40–0		1919	Fitchburg	12–0
1895	Fitchburg	14–6		1920	Fitchburg	35–7
1896	Fitchburg	18–0		1921	Tie	7–7
1897	Fitchburg	4–0		1922	Fitchburg	12–6
1897	Fitchburg	8–0		1924	Fitchburg	48–0
1898	Leominster	5–0		1925	Leominster	9–0
1898	Tie	0–0	**	1926	Fitchburg	20–0
1899	Fitchburg	10–0		1927	Fitchburg	64–0
1899	Tie	0–0		1928	Leominster	6–3
1901	Fitchburg	7–0		1929	Leominster	6–0
1901	Leominster	5–0		1930	Fitchburg	6–0
1903	Leominster	6–0		1931	Fitchburg	24–7
1903	Tie	0–0		1932	Leominster	25–0
1904	Fitchburg	46–0		1933	Fitchburg	20–12
1904	Fitchburg	48–0		1934	Leominster	14–0
1905	Fitchburg	10–0		1935	Fitchburg	33–14
1906	Fitchburg	17–0		1936	Fitchburg	7–6
1907	Tie	4–4		1937	Leominster	26–6
1908	Fitchburg	2–0		1938	Leominster	14–0
1909	Fitchburg	5–0		1939	Leominster	18–0
1910	Leominster	6–0		1940	Leominster	6–0
1910	Leominster	23–0		1941	Fitchburg	14–6
1911	Leominster	9–0		1942	Leominster	25–7
1911	Leominster	17–0		1943	Leominster	13–6
1912	Tie	0–0		1944	Leominster	26–0
1912	Leominster	19–0		1945	Tie	6–6
1913	Tie	0–0		1946	Fitchburg	7–6
1913	Fitchburg	13–0		1947	Fitchburg	13–0
1914	Fitchburg	27–0		1948	Fitchburg	13–7
1914	Fitchburg	33–0		1949	Leominster	26–20
1915	Fitchburg	62–0		1950	Leominster	19–13
1915	Fitchburg	13–0		1951	Fitchburg	12–0
1916	Fitchburg	49–0		1952	Leominster	20–7
1916	Fitchburg	27–0		1953	Leominster	7–0
1917	Fitchburg	42–0		1954	Leominster	27–7

1955	Leominster	39–7	1995	Fitchburg	38–6
1956	Leominster	44–13	1996	Fitchburg	28–19
1957	Fitchburg	20–14	1997	Leominster	26–8
1958	Fitchburg	24–10	1998	Fitchburg	21–7
1959	Tie	0–0	1999	Fitchburg	38–21
1960	Tie	14–14	2000	Fitchburg	28–6
1961	Leominster	26–12	2001	Fitchburg	26–14
1962	Leominster	14–0	2002	Fitchburg	28–20
1963	Fitchburg	20–0	2003	Fitchburg	24–14
1964	Fitchburg	12–8	2004	Leominster	19–14
1965	Leominster	27–0	2005	Leominster	20–6
1966	Leominster	14–12	2006	Leominster	34–6
1967	Leominster	16–0	2007	Leominster	14–13
1968	Fitchburg	16–14	2008	Fitchburg	20–17
1969	Leominster	40–18	2009	Leominster	21–6
1970	Leominster	14–12			
1971	Fitchburg	12–7			
1972	Fitchburg	27–19			
1973	Leominster	15–0			
1974	Leominster	36–13			
1975	Leominster	19–0			
1976	Leominster	38–22			
1977	Leominster	7–0			
1978	Leominster	3–0			
1979	Leominster	34–6			
1980	Leominster	43–8			
1981	Leominster	27–12			
1982	Leominster	41–6			
1983	Leominster	28–12			
1984	Fitchburg	29–2			
1985	Leominster	13–6			
1986	Leominster	23–15			
1987	Leominster	20–6			
1988	Leominster	25–8			
1989	Leominster	29–6			
1990	Leominster	27–0			
1991	Fitchburg	14–0			
1992	Fitchburg	14–13			
1993	Fitchburg	44–40			
1994	Fitchburg	38–14			

*Not included in series standing or point totals since the game is loosely categorized as a high school match. This game occurred in conjunction with the Leominster Cattle Show on Wednesday, September 13, 1893. Another game between "Fitchburgs and the Leominsters" in November of that year ended with Fitchburg dominating. The score of that game or the composition of the teams is not known.

**The *Fitchburg Sentinel* account claims this game as a 5–0 Fitchburg victory; however, the game official ruled the game a scoreless tie. That result is included in the series standings and point totals.

Series Standings
Fitchburg 58-58-10
Leominster 58-58-10

Point Totals
Fitchburg: 1,683
Leominster: 1,586

The rivalry between Leominster and Fitchburg is not the oldest in the country. Nevertheless it may be the most remarkable football tradition in all of America. On Thanksgiving morning 2009, Fitchburg and Leominster high schools met for the 126th time. Leominster prevailed by a score of 21–6. After 126 games played between the two communities, the standings are even. Each community has won fifty-eight games and the other ten contests ended in a tie. It would be hard to find another football rivalry as old as Leominster and Fitchburg that could claim such a close competition over more than a century. No one could have predicted when it all started that 116 years later neither team could claim supremacy.

Bibliography

I. Archives

    Crocker Field House, Fitchburg, MA
    Fitchburg Historical Society, Fitchburg, MA
    Leominster Historical Society, Leominster, MA
    Leominster Public Library, Valuable Collection, Leominster, MA

II. Primary Sources

    Barnard Bulletin, Columbia University
    Boston Globe
    Boston Herald
    The Boulder (Fitchburg High School Year Book 1934)
    Drake Letter
    Evening Tribune (Alberta, MN)
    Fitchburg Sentinel
    Fitchburg v. Leominster Thanksgiving Day Program, 1933
    Leominster Enterprise
    Los Angeles Times
    The Magnet (Leominster High School Year Book 1933)
    NFL Collective Bargaining Agreement 2006-2012
    New York Times
    Oakland (California) *Sports Tribune*

Official Guide Book of Chicago World's Fair 1934, A Century of Progress, International Exposition

San Mateo Times

Syracuse Herald

USA Today

III. Books

Anderson, Lars. 2007. *Carlisle vs. Army*. New York: Random House.

Bodanza, Mark C. 2009. *A Game That Forged Rivals*. Bloomington, IN: iUniverse.

Bodanza, Mark C. 2004. *The Coming Crucible*. Leominster, MA.

Brinkley, Douglas. 1998. *History of the United States*. New York: Viking Penguin.

Burrough, Bryan. 2004. *Public Enemies: America's Greatest Crime Wave and the Birth of the FBI, 1933-1934*. New York: The Penguin Press.

Collison, Gary. 1997. *Shadrach Minkins, From Fugitive Slave to Citizen*. Cambridge, MA: Harvard University Press.

Farley, James A. 1938. *Behind the Ballots*. New York: Harcourt Brace.

Hand, Jack. 1966. *Great Running Backs of the NFL*. New York: Random House.

Kirkpatrick, Denis. 1971. *The City and the River*. Fitchburg, MA: Fitchburg Historical Society.

Little, Lou and Arthur Sampson. 1934. *Lou Little's Football*. Leominster, MA: Leominster Printing Co.

Meltzer, Milton. 1991. *Brother, Can You Spare A Dime?* New York: Facts on File, Inc.

Montville, Leigh. 2006. *The Big Bam: The Life and Times of Babe Ruth*. New York: Doubleday.

Oates, Bob, Jr., ed. 1969. *The First Fifty Years: The Story of the National Football League*. New York: Simon and Schuster.

Okeson, William R., ed. 1933. *Spalding's Official Football Rules of the National Collegiate Athletic Association, 1933*. New York: American Sports Publishing.

Okeson, William R., ed. 1934. *Spalding's Official Football Rules of the National Collegiate Athletic Association, 1934.* New York: American Sports Publishing.

Piascik, Andy. 2007. *The Best Show in Football.* Lanham, MD: Taylor Trade Publishing.

Poole, Gary Andrew. 2008. *The Galloping Ghost, Red Grange.* Boston: Houghton Mifflin Company.

Roosevelt, Franklin D. 1933-1950. Roseman, Samuel I., ed. *Public Papers and Addresses, 13 Vols.* New York: Random House, Macmillan, Harper & Brothers.

Smith, Jean, Edward. 2007. *FDR.* New York: Random House.

Treat, Roger. 1979. *The Encyclopedia of Football: 16th Revised Edition.* South Brunswick and New York: A.S. Barnes and Company.

Watterson, John Sayle. 2002. *College Football.* Baltimore: JHU Press.

Whittingham, Richard. 2001. *Rites of Autumn: The Story of College Football.* New York: The Free Press.

IV. Additional Sources

The Leaders, Breaking Racial Barriers in the NFL, DVD. Produced by Steve Sabot. 2007. NFL Productions LLC.

1934 Football Team, http://bentley.umich.edu/athdept/football/fbteam/1934.

The Original Public Enemy, http://www.johndillinger.com/about-john-dillinger-menu-33/original-public-enemy.

The Rivalry, DVD. Directed and produced by Jack Celli and Carl Piermarini, Leominster, MA, Originally released in 1983 and updated in 2005. Piermacelli Films, Inc.

Timeline of FBI History, http://www.tbi.gov/libref/historic/history/historicdates.htm.

Wolff, Alexander. "The Jackie Robinson of the NFL." *Sports Illustrated III* (October 17, 2009).

Index

Bold indicates photos. *t* indicates
tables.

Breinigsville, PA USA
07 November 2010
248814BV00002B/4/P